AF506150

In Human Presence—Hope

With deep affection to
    M. Forest Ashbrook,
    my father, who demonstrated a way of ministering

With deep appreciation to
    South Congregational Church
    Rochester, New York
    First Baptist Church
    Granville, Ohio
    parishes that became occasions of ministry

In
Human
Presence—
Hope

JAMES B. ASHBROOK

JUDSON PRESS, Valley Forge

IN HUMAN PRESENCE—HOPE

Reproduced from Palma Bucarelli, **Alberto Giacometti,** ed. Editalia, 1962, Rome, and used by permission.

Acknowledgments

Most of all, I am indebted to those individuals and groups who have allowed me to share their hurts and hopes through the years of my professional life. I do not name them even within the context of the sympathetic interpretation of this book; the names used are fictitious in order to respect each person's right to reticence and to universalize the experiences shared. Yet my gratitude is great.

The systematic development of the orienting compass discussed in chapters twelve and thirteen has been disclosed by extended conversation with Donald E. O'Hair, John D. Martin, Jr., Robert L. Carrigan, and Gerald B. Evans.

Chapter eleven, on experience at the divinity school and my interpretation, has been clarified by the critical comments of John Walker, Stanley Skinner, and Thomas Troeger. In addition, I have been helped in my understanding of racism by conversations with my colleagues John David Cato and Henry H. Mitchell.

Portions of chapters three, four, seven, and eight originally appeared in *Pastoral Psychology* in February, 1966; May, 1970; October, 1957; and September, 1969, respectively, and have been revised extensively for this volume. Chapter six originally appeared as "When a Sermon Backfires" in *The Pulpit,* December, 1959, vol. 30, no. 12. Portions of chapter nine originally appeared in

Religion in Life in the Spring, 1970, issue (Copyright © 1970 by Abingdon Press). An earlier and more detailed account of the experience described in chapter eleven appeared as "A New Day Has Taken Place: An Interpretive Case Description of the Crisis in Black-and-White" in the *Journal of Human Relations,* 1969, vol. 17.

My wife, Patricia, and James E. Dittes made editorial suggestions, which have added to whatever clarity I have managed to achieve. Harold L. Twiss encouraged me to undertake this project and provided the support necessary to complete it.

My gratitude to Colgate Rochester/Bexley Hall/Crozer is considerable. Dean of the Faculty, George B. Hall, encouraged me in the project and provided time for its pursuit. The secretarial staff of Mrs. Karen Evans, Mrs. Hazel Spaven, Mrs. Sylvia Haygood, Mrs. Elizabeth Gordon, and Mrs. Katherine Bishop, under the direction of Mrs. Joanne Oliver, labored patiently and diligently with my illegible scribble and my disorganized state.

To each and all I am deeply grateful. Whatever insight this book conveys is in large measure due to others. Whatever inadequacy it perpetrates is in large measure due to myself.

J. B. A.

Rochester, New York
June 1, 1971.

Contents

having-to-be-in-this-world

"Yes, I do find a change in the public. Instead of reading their future they now prefer me to reminisce nostalgically over their past."

Two fortune tellers conversing over tea

New Yorker cartoon

". . . We've got to live, no matter how many skies have fallen."

D. H. Lawrence [1]

Why This Book

Why this book?

Frankly, I am writing it for myself. I want to pull together fragments of experience and glimpses of understanding. I want to see what I have been immersed in during these last twenty years of professional pilgrimage. I want to sketch the contours of this pilgrimage more clearly. I want to share its deep satisfactions and its equally deep frustrations. I suspect, though, that most importantly of all, I am writing it because I have invested the bulk of my time in people and now I desire to put some of that living on paper, where it will stay put.

Clearly, I am writing for concerned colleagues who are in the pastorate. Daily they push their way through accumulating trivia, overwhelming complexity, and unrelenting perplexity. Individual need cries out for healing. Social necessity screeches for attention.

Broken persons, breaking world; breaking persons, broken world.

How do pastors change that which can be changed? How can they accept that which is constant? How do they distinguish the changeable from the unchangeable?

Moreover, the pain of personal need and the agony of social necessity are not confined to concerned pastors alone. These conditions aggravate, irritate, and threaten every sensitive person, regardless of one's occupational responsibility. People are apt to clutch desperately at any straw of focus that may be swirling past. Thus, I write for the perturbed and searching nonprofessional as well.

Quite self-consciously, I put these chapters out with the fear that they are mere fragments. While there is an implicit integrity and even much explicit integration, I want to retain the process quality of the material. I am sharing with you bits and pieces of personal and professional living that have forced me to think. I have had to struggle to assimilate these fragments for my own spiritual survival as well as for my psychological growth and my professional development. A ragged right-hand margin will suggest the fragmentary nature of the bits of life that I will be describing in some parts of the book. These experiences and their reflection cover the last two decades of agonizing with what becoming human and humanizing humanity are all about.

Some of the material is quite intimate. You may feel that I have been too intimate; yet I want to convey to you as much of the sense of my self and my search as is appropriate. While I can and do distinguish my private world from my public world, nevertheless, the truth is that my person and my profession are inextricably intertwined.

Some of the material is quite general. Therein you may feel that I have been too abstract. Yet I want to put out for your reactions the guiding principles and orientation I have come to rely on. While I cherish my private world, I am heavily invested in my professional task. I struggle to make sense of life both for myself and others.

The more theoretical and technical material comes at the end. It has been primarily in the last two years that my present state of understanding has crystallized. Thus, such material belongs at the end, both logically and chronologically.

You might consider the chapters that follow as replaceable inserts in a loose-leaf notebook on the subject of change and constancy. By that I mean that I have selected—somewhat arbitrarily from a multitude of experienced events—a few experiences that suggest directions *for* understanding even as they have proven to be applications *of* understanding. These range from those that have been more personal and intimate through the more pastoral and congregational to the more institutional and structural. Other experienced events will replace these as the flood of change continues. In this respect, understanding must always be regarded as an open process. It can never be a finished product.

The frontispiece is a picture of a sculptured work by Alberto Giacometti entitled *Three Men Walking*. I shall be referring to this from time to time. After World War II, Giacometti's style shifted to these thin, elongated figures, stabbing space with the poignant loneliness of the human being. For him, we do not move

> according to a constant or predictable direction or rhythm. . . . On the contrary, we walk and we grope for each other in the darkness; we never know if we are close or far. . . .[1]

Although his figures live in "an unsurpassable distance and appear "unreachable," [2] Giacometti conveys hope by means of human presence:

> There is something: our substance, our miserable, meaningless, yet necessary human reality; a substance and a reality more *lasting* than the substance and reality of things, a small bit of substance and of reality that the vacuum cannot devour and absorb and, on the contrary, is choked by it, as if by a stone in the throat. . . . our human substance, even more now that it comes out of a struggle against the abstractness of space, is certainly not a great thing, but in the meantime saves us and allows us to make a gesture, to continue in our existence.[3]

In a day when everything has torn loose and little if anything may really be simple, we need more than kind hearts and clean hands. We reel from a future that arrives ahead of schedule. We stagger from an accelerating stream of surprises that tests our capacity for coping.[4] We fight against principalities and powers—structures and institutions, transpersonal forces—that resist good intentions and intuitive hunches. That is why we need clear minds and right tools. That is why we need planned change for meaningful constancy.

Yet, in the end, our alienation from human experience "will not yield to a mere reshuffling of our society's institutional structures."[5] What frees us, insists Theodore Roszak in reflecting on the technocratic society and the search for a counter culture, "must be primarily therapeutic in character and not merely institutional." [6] Thus, for me, Giacometti's figures are symbols of our human pain and heralds of genuine hope: people and paths, gestures and growth, substance and search, stubborn constancy and flowing change. Here, surely, is hope because of human presence!

One

Is There Anything to Go On?

Instant change—forced change—resented change—demanded change—desired change—planned change—intended change—resisted change—relentless change—continual change—change—change—change—

A New England farmer expressed the widespread sentiment about change:

"My grandfather knew the number of whiskers in the Almighty's beard.
He knew what it was that makes a rock or a table.
I don't even know what happened yesterday, let alone tomorrow.
I don't even understand the formula that says nobody knows. We've got nothing to go on—got no way to think about things." [1]

No wonder people feel uptight, frightened, timid, resentful, vindictive, at loose ends, all in pieces.

We suffer from what Alvin Toffler labels "future shock"—a convergence of acceleration plus novelty plus diversity. We recoil from the head-on collision between the pressure to live at an ever faster pace, adapting more rapidly, making and breaking ties with people and places oftener, and making swifter decisions and the just as powerful counter-pressures of novelty and diversity which demand that we process more data, that we break out of

19

our old, carefully honed routines, that we examine each situation anew before we make a decision.[2]

STABILITY VERSUS FLEXIBILITY

One man's private fantasy portrays many people's experience. In response to a request to let come into his mind whatever was lurking in the shadows, "he rapidly produced two mythological pictures." In the first he saw himself in "a kind of medieval castle, closely guarded" and completely unwilling to come out into the open world. In the second he felt like "a man clutching a post in the middle of a swirling stream that threatened to carry him away." [3]

Like that man, we either retreat into an entrenched and immovable position or we feel at the mercy of a raging flood. Either way, we are confronted with the dilemma of survival: stability versus flexibility.

Constancy and change are the twin poles around which everything moves. Constancy is something that must be sought as well as rejected. Change is something that must be resisted as well as encouraged. By understanding the interplay between stability and flexibility, we can shape change for human purposes.

Clearly, we need means of balancing change and constancy. Clearly, we need to meet the threat of chaos with firmness and the threat of rigidity with flexibility. Clearly, we need to learn when to loosen our hold on what has been and when to tighten our grip on what might be. Clearly, we need both a focused change and an adaptive constancy.

But what constitutes focused change? What comprises adaptive constancy? How do we know the difference between change that is focused and change that is frantic? How do we distinguish between constancy that is adaptive and constancy that is maladaptive?

Now I would be kidding myself and misleading you if I believed that I had *the* answer to focused change and adaptive constancy.

The entire biblical witness couples the *already* of constancy with the *not yet* of change. "It does not yet appear what we shall be. . . ." When Reality bursts forth in its fullness, we shall be taken completely by surprise. At best we see through a glass dimly.[4]

No one has the answer: life is too fluid, too fascinating, too frustrating, too full!

There have been months at a time when I have felt empty, lost, and bewildered by what was going on inside of me and what was taking place around me. Nothing seemed to hang together with anything else. I had no handle with which to grab hold of experience and shape events. I felt bewildered at best, and crushed at worst.

But there have also been other times when I have experienced fleeting moments of ecstatic insight. Everything was of a pattern. I knew how to make sense and move ahead. Everything had a place and everything was in its place. I saw the meaning and knew the means.

Out of that fluctuation between confusion and clarity I have found some clues about constancy and change. I have discovered —to my comfort—that my confusion is seldom as chaotic as I have felt it to be. I have learned—to my chagrin—that my clarity is never as focused as I have believed it to be. Nevertheless, clues, hints, hunches, directions, suggestions, patterns, and possibilities continue to emerge from reflection upon ongoing experience. These dimly perceived realities are taking on increasing shape. Even though I know that my insightful *understanding is limited,* I also know that *I am seeing.*

THE IMPLICIT AND THE EXPLICIT

In contrast with that Maine farmer, I believe we do have something to go on. There are helpful ways of thinking about life. All cannot be said to be random. All is not mystery. Experience, when reflected upon, does provide insight into what is happening. From the fragments in this book I have begun to see not Reality, if there is any such objective entity, but reality as it lives and breathes in individuals, groups, and institutional structures.

In working through these events, many times I followed only intuitive or, more accurately, instinctive hunches. Often I simply blundered through. Occasionally, more clearly I saw forces at work. Now I am convinced that what was implicit in these separate experiences can be understood more explicitly. There is an underlying sense to what takes place between persons and among groups. That sense, obviously, can never be perfect, yet it does provide a vehicle for meaning. It enables us to approach change with understanding rather than with bewilderment. It allows us to learn from experience rather than be battered by it.

We exercise dominion and authority over the created world by ordering experience and events in meaningful ways. We language—name—what *is,* whether that be classifying parts of the physical environment as with Adam's labeling every living creature, or identifying aspects of our psychic world as with the Gerasene demoniac's labeling his fractured personality as Legion. Various theological doctrines provide a base on which to build our understanding:

> The doctrine of Creation takes seriously the "what's there" of human *existence.*
>
> The doctrine of Logos takes seriously the "felt meaning of what's there" of *human* existence.
>
> The doctrine of redemption takes seriously the responsibility for making actual the human *potential.*
>
> The doctrine of ministry sets the meaning and task of becoming genuinely human within the context of a community of faith and with focus upon representative *leadership* in that community.

Whether we start with the most general construct of God or with the most specific instance of an individual, the dynamics of finding whether there is anything to go on appear similar. We move back and forth between what we regard as constant and what we find as changing. We seek to find what is permanent in the midst of the passing. We endeavor to keep the passing from contaminating the permanent.

CERTAINTY VERSUS SIGNIFICANCE

For me, one of the greatest perplexities of constancy and change lies in the tension between the general and the specific. For example, what we can say of a group is seldom, if ever, what we can say of an individual. How we characterize an individual is seldom, if ever, how we would characterize a group.

Gordon Allport highlighted the predicament by quoting what Sherlock Holmes said to his friend Dr. Watson:

> While the individual man is an insoluble puzzle, in the aggregate he becomes a mathematical certainty. You can never foretell what any one man will do, but you can say with precision what an average number will be up to. Individuals vary but percentages remain constant.[5]

General certainty on the one side and particular significance on the other—such is the dialectical continuum and perpetual dilemma. The more sweeping our remarks the more confident we feel, yet the more likely we are to be wrong about specific instances. The more careful our observations the more sense they make, yet the more likely we are to be missing the larger focus.

When certainty and significance are viewed as opposites, we discover an inverse relationship between them. The more accurately we describe an individual situation, the less able we are to generalize our understanding to other situations; the more encompassing our general analysis, the less adequate it is to take account of the peculiarities of any particular situation. When we deal with the universal, we gain certainty but lose significance. When we limit ourselves to the unique, we gain significance but lose certainty.

When certainty and significance are understood as necessary complements, however, we experience the creative interplay between them.

In terms of constancy and certainty, we avoid the sweeping generalization that is cut off from any specific situation. We give up wandering anywhere and everywhere by gearing in somewhere. We resist the temptation to say something about everything. We periodically attend to the quivering living particular.

In terms of change and significance, we avoid the isolated particular that prevents our generalizing to other situations. We try to see in what ways seemingly unrelated experiences are similar and in what ways they are different. We resist the temptation to string together unrelated illustrations. We continually search for the more embracing pattern.

I have sat in the midst of the experiences and events described in this book. I have allowed their nuances of meaning to impress themselves upon me. There is something about them completely independent of what I might like them to be. They have their own order, whether I can express it or not.

At the same time I have come at these experiences and events with a certain mind set. Even though I have tried to be receptively open, my understanding has been patterned, in part, by my purposes, my interests, my background, and my experience.

As time has passed, my experience has accumulated and my reflection has been refined. I have begun to construct a pattern of systematic organization. I have disciplined my impressionistic hunches by analyzing relationships and reducing contradictions.

Theory and practice have played back and forth. (I spell out the resulting fusion in the last two chapters.) Constancy and change have informed each other. Certainty has led to significance; significance has fostered certainty.

In part because of Bonhoeffer, we now conceive of ministry as *being for others*.[6] Traditionally, being for others has tended to be restricted to ministry to individuals as individuals. Currently, being for others tends to be associated with ministry also to power structures, apart from individuals. No ministry can be whole ministry that does not take into account both persons and structures. Only thus can we be for others in ways that are humanly relevant, organizationally realistic, and socially appropriate.

Anyone engaged in ministry knows how slippery certainty and significance are. He knows the subtle relationship between what is working quietly and unnoticed in a situation and what he brings to and presses upon that situation. He knows the painfully delicate balancing between the order in keeping things stable and the change in allowing flexibility.

It is so with my experiences and reflections. Most of them fit together. Some of them do not. That is the nature of understanding. Such must be the format of my contribution to comprehending change and constancy.

able-to-be-in-this-world

In the first legend of the Grail,
it is said that
      the Grail . . . belongs to
      the first comer who asks
      the guardian of the vessel,
      a king three-quarters
      paralyzed by the most
      painful wound,

"WHAT ARE YOU GOING THROUGH?"
Simone Weil [1]

Two

Ordeal with Chaos: The Turmoil of a Disturbed Boy

One autumn, we took a four-year-old boy into our home. It sounds so simple. We had believed it would be that simple. But never has the issue of change pressed so acutely. Never have we struggled so unceasingly to comprehend. Never have we been so unable to get relief from the onslaught of chaos.

Prior to that, my wife and I had had wide experience with disturbed adults. We had absorbed the hurts and scarring of a variety of relationships. While the effects of earlier battles were apparent, the clash of conflict remained but a distant din.

Our own children bore the scars of our anxieties. They equally showed evidences of our health. We could see the life force transforming life's pains into the very stuff of human becoming.

Upsets—yes; disruptions—no!

Conflict—yes; clash—no!

Frustrations—yes; fear—no!

We knew who we were. We knew who they were. Even in our differences and our distances we experienced our wholeness and our intimacy.

THE CONVULSIVE EXPERIENCE

We thought another child would be just that—another child.

Oh, we knew his life had been hard. We suspected our comfortable closeness would have to modify. We anticipated a normal period of readjustment. In brief, we affirmed that our love was strong enough to share. And only as we shared that love could we have that love.

Initial Onslaught

Our excitement at the challenge disintegrated in the face of raw terror, mobilized mistrust, and organized destructiveness. For terror, mistrust, and destructiveness blasted us from the first moments of contact. All too rapidly we learned that love is not enough. Only in retrospect did we understand the meaning of "affect indigestion," namely, that open acceptance and spontaneous affection generate fear rather than allay it. When the only relationship a child has known has been destructive, then *every* relationship, no matter how positive, looms as a menacing reality to be attacked and destroyed.

Those first weeks are a nightmare to recall. Although Ronald was four years old, he acted as a two-year old. We had been told he was mentally retarded. He came with a six-word vocabulary. Later, we learned that those who had been taking care of him had not prepared him for his coming to live with us.

The catalog of behavioral reactions that bombarded us is unbelievable:

- —The littlest demand precipitated screeching, raging, kicking, and destructiveness; he had *no* frustration tolerance.
- —Verbal communication consisted of shrieking "No's," growls, or screams; he could not put two words together in any form.
- —He raced around in a frenzy, his feet tripping, his head and eyes rolling wildly.
- —When thwarted, he injured himself by such methods as jamming his hand into small places, scratching himself, tearing his clothes, and even trying to push out his own eye.
- —In moments of rage he destroyed any available object, whether it was a box, or a book, or his own special "treasure."
- —Every morning his bed and pajamas were soaked with perspiration; he lived in perpetual panic of the unknown and the unexpected.
- —He demanded to be fed instantly and would wolf down

enormous amounts of foods, only to demand more, as though
he could never be sure that there would be another meal.
—He refused to get out of the car when we went anywhere,
for fear that he would be deserted.
—The sound or sight of a dog unleashed raw terror, the result
(we later learned) of his having been bitten in the stomach
by a large dog.
—Candles on a birthday cake set off raw terror, the result
(we later learned) of two traumatic experiences with fire.
—When touched, his body would become as rigid as that of
a corpse; when spanked, he gave no sign of feeling; when
hurt, he went into hysterical panic.
—His attention span was nonexistent; he could not sit
quietly to listen to a story or to watch television.
—When crossed, he impulsively and viciously scratched our
children, us, furniture, and rugs like an enraged cat.
—He constantly poked, touched, and felt our ears, noses, and
mouths.

I can hardly absorb this catalog of horrors. Yet I know
these behaviors occurred, for I am writing from notes made at
the time. Even so, the experience still seems unbelievable.

After a few months the self-injury diminished. We eventually
refused to be horrified. Horror no longer had the power to
manipulate us. The profuse perspiring ceased. Muscular rigidity
relaxed. Motor control improved. Words began to appear. A
slight tolerance for fire took root. The discomfort at going into
strange places grew more endurable. Yet the rage and
destructiveness persisted. When he was not destroying something
in tirades of anger, he talked incessantly of wanting to do so.

Then hyperkinetic activity appeared. Hmmmm! Hmmmmm!
Hmmmmmm! It would start early in the morning and continue
unabated until he was in bed at night. His "motor" ran all the
time.

This "Hiroshima" left my wife and me without visible and
viable ways of living, relating, and responding. Old certainties
of understanding-love crashed. To recognize his feelings and
to limit his actions had no discernible effect. Our reservoir
of affection abruptly ran dry. Even my clinical acumen dissolved
in the acid of lightning attack and unrelenting wanton destruction.
We got so caught up in the turmoil that we failed to provide

breathing spaces necessary for distance. Not only were we impotent in the presence of this alien other; even more, we felt ourselves losing our own creative past.

Ministering Children

A little child will lead them. So says the Bible. So it was with us.

Our own children, ages three, five, nine, and eleven at the time, began to find their way through and to show us a way through. For them, each day was a new day, even as each hour was a new hour. For us, each day was an extension of the nightmare, even as each hour accentuated the horror. They showed us how a person could be viciously attacked one moment and be caringly accepting the next. They showed us how they could be themselves, define the limits beyond which they would not be pushed, and in the same act affirm the reality of the other person.

Not only did they demonstrate a direction, but also they unrelentingly exposed our limitations.

Ten weeks after Ronald's arrival, our five-year-old asked, "Mommy, why is it everyone in our family has accepted Ronald except you and Daddy?"

Months later, she inquired, "How do bad people come to be bad?"

When told they usually grew up in families where they were unloved and not encouraged to be themselves, she asked, "Would Ronald have grown up to be a bad person if he hadn't come to live with us?"

"Probably."

"And will he grow up that way now?"

From such penetrating innocence we were reminded of our resolves *and* our forgetfulness.

Our nine-year-old has been the most open of the family in drawing upon the strength of religious resources. One day when she had been left in charge (an unfortunate premature decision on our part), Ronald erupted. During such moments we had found it necessary to isolate him until the full force of his fury subsided and his discriminating ego could function again. She removed him to his room and closed the door. He insisted upon opening it. She held it shut; he battered it with blocks. It takes little imagination to feel for her as well as for him.

Of all the children, she experienced the most sympathy and expressed the most understanding. Her own spirit throbbed whenever he had to be restrained or disciplined. Yet in that particular moment *she* had to restrain his fury while simultaneously she felt his pain.

Later she reported, "All the time I held on to that door I prayed to God in my heart to give me the strength to hold on. I knew that was what had to be done. But, oh, it was hard!"

In such moments we were reminded of resources beyond our own. She showed us how to hold together hurt and hope, limits and love, practice and prayer. Our family life slowly reshaped. Each of us began to experience and express new roles and new responsibilities.

THE SEARCH FOR UNDERSTANDING

Our initial hope lay in getting him to a child psychiatrist. Play therapy—that was the answer! Straighten him out! Work through the trauma! Mold him into a recognizable human being! The hope crumbled at the moment we met with the therapist.

Ronald was *too* disturbed! The foundation that was necessary for therapy even to begin did not exist. So diffuse was his sense of self that he could not enter fruitfully into an intensified relationship that encouraged expression or demanded exploration. He lacked qualities basic to human becoming!

We could no longer think of the problem as "that child." Now we had to explore our own situation: "Who are *we?*" Now we had to determine "What do *we* do?"

The therapist kept our heads above water. He enabled us to modify our expectations. He pointed to change that was vaguely discernible in the smoke of the bombardment. He helped us to live with the uglier aspects of our personalities that were exposed by Ronald's blitzkrieg. He encouraged us to differentiate who we were, who our own children were, and who Ronald was. He guided us to evolve clearer responsibilities for the new relationships.

Unless suffering can take on meaning, it destroys. Unless understanding emerges, disintegration takes over.
But where was the meaning? What was the understanding? What sense was there in this "senseless" cyclone? Where was

the rationality in such "irrational" behavior? How were we to transform the whirlwind into a gentle breeze?

At first these questions poured out. We ached for answers. We talked incessantly. I read voraciously. As life's inner ordering began to reassert itself, "answers" started to be lived. Even so, unfinished feelings and fragments of shattered being continued to torture.

As reflective adults, we sought to understand. As responsible persons, we longed for right attitudes and appropriate behavior. What did the "experts" have to say? Were there theoretical orientations and practical insights for this unknown experience?

Psychoanalytic Theory

Melanie Klein was the outstanding British child psychoanalyst. I bypassed her. She saw all behavior as symbolic of underlying psychosexual conflict.[1] Except for unusual interest of a primitive kind in bowel movements and urinating, Ronald could hardly be understood that way. Even the preoedipal mother relationship, so essential for the Oedipal conflict to develop, had not been experienced by him.

I turned next to Anna Freud, probably the most outstanding of all child analysts.

In terms of Ronald, Anna Freud presented little clarity. Her insistence that such a child be removed from the family (in this instance, even his adopting family) and incorporated into an isolated and protected relationship with an analyst was impossible. Neither a facility nor funds were available.

Just as limiting was her theoretical viewpoint. The process of loosening and binding impulses is basically rational, that is, giving a child insight into his mechanisms of defense. Such insight depends, according to the theory, upon an affectionate tie between analyst and child.[2] Ronald could not establish an affectionate tie with anyone. He was insulated and isolated. His very disturbance reflected primitive deficiency in the organization of the ego, which itself precluded insight into mechanisms of defense.

I turned away from psychoanalytical thinking. Its theory left only an untrustworthy emotional base, a destructive environmental setting, and disruptive ongoing relationships. Its practical implications had no practical possibilities.

Relational Differentiation

My next move brought me back into the ongoingness of everyday living. Frederick Allen, formerly director of the Philadelphia Child Guidance Clinic, had lived out and thought through what has come to be known as a philosophy of responsible participation and relationalism.[3] His thinking can be suggested by these five points:

1. Human beings develop in an orderly way. The development moves from the undifferentiated unity of the organism with its environment, through the experience of separation and differentiation, into the experience of functional interrelatedness. Ultimate value, therefore, lies in personal relationships.

2. The human organism is a unity and not a duality. The self does not eternally fight against itself. The qualities of spontaneity, health, and creativity come from finding the growing differentiated life *within* the person himself.

3. Limits are positive, not negative. By recognizing and using limits, a person experiences meaning. Life is simultaneously differentiated *and* related. Only through interaction with that which is other than oneself does a differentiated and freely functioning self emerge. The therapist uses limits as an instrument for growth, not as a weapon for personal aggrandizement.

4. The therapeutic relationship focuses on the immediate, living interaction of two human beings. There is no place for an active expert and a passive patient. Allen's philosophy of responsibility requires the child to discover that *"he* can change and not *be changed."* [4] Without ignoring the sources of disturbance, what matters is the present and real encounter with the therapist as a human being.

5. The therapeutic experience is only an extension of everyday experience. "Therapy is an awakening process, but if the waking up is not in the world of immediate reality of people and events, it is not a waking up but a new medium to continue a dream existence." [5]

This position of relational differentiation commended itself to us. Therapy did not need to be confined to one hour or to any number of hours. It must not be restricted to a special person, no matter how helpful he might be. Everything that occurred in the child's world, every relationship which he experienced, could be utilized in the process of differentiation and responsibility.

Ronald's fighting back, frustrating as it might be, could be respected. While we were not to melt before his blasts, neither were we to destroy the source of their strength. His very resistance came to be seen as positive.

Every confrontation carried possibility for clarifying the relationship. Every encounter held promise for discovering a strength that did not destroy. Every experience possessed ingredients for therapeutic change.

Whereas the content of knowledge had been foremost, now the process of knowing took on significance. Whereas the specifics of communication had been uppermost, now the shared attempt at communicating became worthwhile. Even though his behavior seemed "senseless," if we looked closely and listened attentively, we began to sense *some* sense.

Ronald's play provided clues. In play he sought to manage the inundating anxiety. Through play he searched for predictable experience.

For months he pushed boxes, cars, and any movable object around the house with the accompanying noise of roaring engines. Gradually we fathomed this "senseless" frenzy to be a manifestation of his aggression against an environment that had uprooted him. Gradually we appreciated this as an anxious and endless search for a "place" where he would belong.

After nine months he peppered us with questions about gifts he received from us: "Who gave me the turtles?"

"Mommy and daddy did."

"Why you give me the turtles? Why?"

Again and again and again we explained, "We thought Ronald would like them."

"Why you give me birthday party? Why?"

"It was Ronald's birthday. We thought he would like it."

By such questioning Ronald was saying "thank you." He had no other means of spontaneously expressing joy and gratitude. These tangible gifts—to him, symbols of caring—did more to lay the foundation of a relationship than any words we uttered. Solid evidence of interest in him, regardless of his unpleasant behavior, began to leave its mark. He was seeking to make "sense" of *our* "senseless" behavior, even as we were of his!

As time passed, we set firmer restrictions on his behavior. Such restrictions no longer *felt* negative to us, a last desperate reflex at the moment of utter frustration. Although the uneasy feeling never disappeared completely, limits did come to be viewed as vital to growth.

To limit was to care.

To care was to limit.

Only as Ronald found that he could not obliterate the world, could he start to discover himself. By limiting his behavior, we protected him and us from his own destructiveness. By limiting his behavior, we freed him to experience his fear, his anger, his strength—himself.

Thanks to Allen, the inner order of life reappeared. But the basic problem still remained. Ronald had not yet developed to the point at which Allen began. Allen wrote of youngsters who had already experienced some differentiation. They hungered for relationship. Their experience of separation followed upon their experience of closeness. Ronald began with the experience of separation—more accurately, alienation—and not with the experience of closeness. For him, undifferentiated unity had been a reality only within the womb. His differentiation came from initial distance and disturbed communication. That was what made life so distorted and so destructive.

The necessary and sufficient conditions of empathic warmth and genuine congruence had never been present, even in embryonic form. Thus, I delved further.

Ego-Repair and Superego Surgery

Ten years earlier I had worked with a few teenagers who had been similarly disturbed. I vaguely recalled their hate-filled explosiveness. I turned again to the thinking of Fritz Redl and David Wineman, whose works had helped me at the time.[6] I found a sharpened extension of Allen's insight about differentiated relationalism. Previously I had been casually curious; now I was desperately eager.

Let me put their understanding in the following propositions:

1. Children who hate have been deprived of the basic links in human becoming, namely, identification, imaginative expression, and meaningful relatedness. Because these are absent, the ego cannot exercise its reality-function properly. These children, therefore, cannot utilize regular and traditional means of help. They

are "beyond the reach of education." They are "below the grip of the psychiatric interview." Adult interference in disruptive behavior prevents the development of a relationship necessary for such a method to work.

2. The "delinquent ego" issues from the effect of such primary deprivation. We were not dealing with a "weak" ego, for, in point of fact, the ego of the child who hates is adroit in its ability to evade guilt feelings in its search for delinquent encouragement and in its defense against change and change agents. However, the ego cannot perform its necessary functions of giving danger signals, of doing what it intends, of relating appropriately to reality, of establishing a reasonable balance among the "parts" of the personality. In effect, the control system has collapsed, being replaced by the impulse system.

3. Without an adequately functioning ego, the controls of the superego and the conscience cannot develop. Thus, alongside a delinquent ego stands a delinquent conscience. Lack of identification with caring persons leaves the children who hate no "readying" experiences for relating to other adults. Whenever the warning system did function, it functioned solely in post-action evaluation, and then only fleetingly.

4. Only a total treatment approach could touch this "ordeal with chaos." That meant creating a psychologically hygienic environment, programmed for ego support and the clinical exploitation of everyday events. Programs, relationships, and settings *all* had to foster ego control. That meant evolving specific "techniques for the antiseptic manipulations of surface behavior"— around-the-clock considerations not really developed by those who do not have to live with hate-filled children hour after hour, day after day.

5. Purposeful interference and structural support are set within the larger framework of "tax-free love and gratification grants." Relationships with adults have to be unconditional. Activities have to be satisfying. Affection and activity are prerequisites for growth, not rewards of growth.

Their insights came through. Unlike the exclusive and insulated relatedness of Anna Freud, Redl and Wineman underscored the necessary factor of widening relationships. Unlike the restricted interview setting, they spoke of a total treatment milieu. Even as they tolerated symptom expression, so they demanded preventive *and* protective interference. Unlike the therapies that built upon an already established differentiated self, they saw their first task as ego-repair. Only subsequently could they perform superego surgery. In these ways they spoke to our situation.

Their techniques helped us be more systematically therapeutic. The very attempt to think of ego-repair and superego surgery gave us the psychological distance that was crucial to counterbalance personal resentment and retaliation. Let me list some of the more useful strategies: [7]

1. Programming as a full-fledged therapeutic tool
   a. Impulse drainage channels for harmless discharge or satisfactory sublimation
   b. Frustration avoidance and frustration budgeting
   c. Insertion of depersonalized controls
   d. Protective timing
   e. Manipulation of hangover effects and transitional confusions
   f. Protective and preventive interference
   g. The buildup of satisfaction images as resources
   h. The cultivation of interest-contagion
   i. Widening the experiential range
2. Techniques for the antiseptic manipulation of surface behavior
   a. Planned ignoring
   b. Signal interference when a relationship is still functioning and behavior is not serving complex pathology
   c. Proximity and touch control to quiet
   d. Involvement in interest relationship
   e. Hypodermic affection in the face of anxiety or impulse onrush
   f. Tension decontamination through humor
   g. Hurdle help with "specifically frustrating obstacles connected with some problem-solving situation"
   h. Interpretation of a corrected reality appraisal as interference
   i. Regrouping to break up contagious chains
   j. Restructuring activity when it begins to deteriorate
   k. Direct appeal to the personal relationship
   l. Limitation of space and materials
   m. Antiseptic bouncing
   n. Physical restraint

I have listed these, not because their full meaning is self-evident, but because they are suggestive of possibilities. If you want details, you can go to the source. We found these insights helpful in two ways.

In the first place, we felt reassured. We had utilized almost every technique which they described. While Redl and Wineman had had the benefit of staff, our own resources had enabled us to stumble upon a similar approach. In spite of our "failures" (resentment and emotional retaliation), we had been marshaling ego-repairing techniques within our own total treatment setting.

In the second place, their experience gave us a fresh view of the turmoil. They spurred us on to apply the techniques more systematically. Awareness of ego boundaries aided us in resisting the personal undermining from Ronald's relentless siege.

For children who hate, limits constitute the *sine qua non* of ego support. Without them, self-differentiated relatedness cannot grow. The more "normal" pattern of promises and rewards, delayed gratification and significant accomplishment is emasculated.

What was needed and what we gradually came to was a firm stance on what did and did not go. We directed and led and managed more confidently. That, in turn, constrained Ronald to behave with more conforming obedience. His manipulative pattern gave way in the presence of our more adaptive response.

THROUGH THE CHAOS

In the effort to cope with Ronald, we came to understand disturbed people more clearly. Our initial desperation imperceptibly merged into therapeutic curiosity and eventually grew into a shared humanity.

While my wife and I found ourselves functioning in the respective roles of ego-structuring and ego-supporting, our children provided the fertile soil for growth. Their unconditional acceptance, their unself-conscious limit-defining behavior, their capacity for trust and intimacy, and their expressions of initiative and autonomy provided imitative models for human identification and individual identity.

By the sixth month, Ronald felt free enough from anxiety to talk of the future. "When I grow up, I want to have a farm."

After a tantrum, he commonly insisted, "I'm not a bad boy. Ronald not bad. I don't want to be a baby. I'm big."

After nine months the transformation in Ronald looked impressive. Yet, on a day-to-day basis the demands for "special handling" made the process disheartening. In the midst of the moment, what needed to come seemed to be impossible. Ego-repair and superego surgery went on simultaneously.

During that summer, we spent five weeks in a rented house.

As the summer move drew near, Ronald began wetting his bed
and continued to do so about twice a week thereafter. However,
while we were away, he made but one gesture at striking the
door of his room. There were only two attacks of scratching.
On three occasions he announced, "I need to tear up something"
and then proceeded to rip up tissue boxes that had been
designated for that purpose.

In moments of extreme frustration, that hate-filled, vicious look
reappeared. The destructive threats against our two youngest
children, the house, the automobile, and us continued. Only,
now they had more steam than power.

Reluctantly, he also grew acquainted with dogs. Many times
he could stand quietly next to them. On occasion he even
managed to pet them.

By the end of our first year together Ronald was socialized
enough to enter therapy. Despite sporadic upset, acting-out, and
regression, progress continued. Most of his therapy hour consisted
of playing with clay. He would hammer it, pound it, and smash it.
He would mold it into feces-like shapes and test whether he
could put them on the rug instead of on the linoleum. By the
end of the fall he had grown in his capacity to tolerate realistic
limits.

That winter I went on leave. We lived in another rented house.
It was smaller than our own. Yet at no time did any of the
earlier difficulties arise!

While we were away, we made the biggest decision about
Ronald. A middle-aged, childless couple had adopted Ronald's
older brother and now they wanted to adopt Ronald. Frankly,
we were relieved. We had exhausted ourselves in battle. Our
resiliency had been permanently impaired. We had talked of
keeping him; yet we realized our limitations.

In contrast to his having no preparation for coming to us, we
carefully prepared him for the change. We talked about his
brother. We described his new mother and father. We showed
him pictures. They wrote letters. Then came the day!

As Ronald and I stepped through the door of the big plane,
he turned and waved to our family. That was such a poignant
moment! Even as I write of it six years later, my eyes fill with
tears and my throat chokes with emotion.

We *all* had lived through hell. We *all* had been exhausted by battle. The juggernaut left my wife's sense of self crippled in a way from which she will never fully recover. Nevertheless, in those last two weeks we *all* managed somehow to try to work our way up through the past and remember to forget it. Our wounds went deep; the scars still show; yet my wife and I had come to feel deep respect for that little boy—for his spirit, his strength, and his courage. Almost analogous to Dante in *The Divine Comedy,* he had been guided through purgatory. Now as he moved on into more satisfying spheres, he left his guides behind.

The long plane trip passed uneventfully. As we stepped into the terminal, there stood his brother, his new mother, and his new father. He had found a home!

I stayed with the family for twenty-four hours. We thought this would help the adjustment. Horror of horrors—the family had two nervous French hounds! They pranced around the house and pounced on people unexpectedly. By the time I left, Ronald and his brother lay on the floor between the restless dogs watching television! In so short a time they had become the best of friends.

Since then, the communication between Ronald and us has been little. While we have not agreed with the parents' desire to sever all contact, we have respected their intent. What little we have heard has been encouraging.

Ronald proved to be "a delightful child." They had been starved in their longing to give affection; he was ready to receive affection. With us he always retained a respectful distance. With them he lapped up their emotional and physical warmth. How adaptively reciprocal! In the next fall he entered first grade. The last word was: Continued progress!

Periodically our children reminisce nostalgically, "How wonderful it was when Ronald was with us!" "If only Ronald could come to visit us." They remember the happiness; they have forgotten the hurt—and we are humbled!

Three

Losing One's Mind
and Coming to One's Senses

"What would you feel like if you were a leper?"

I was asking a fifth-grade church school class of which I am a co-teacher. We were discussing the ministry of Jesus and more especially his healing miracles. The discussion had shifted from the act of healing to the experience of being healed. By my question I was trying to get them to experience a little of the radical impact of Jesus' actions.

"Awful! I would feel awful!" acknowledged one.

"Dirty," said another. "Dirty and filthy."

"Nobody would want to be near me. I would feel all alone. Nobody would like me. Everyone would be disgusted by me."

"And what must the leper have felt like," I asked, referring to the passages in Mark 1:40-45; Matthew 8:2-4; Luke 5:12-16, "when Jesus reached out and touched him, putting his hand on his hand like this?" As I asked, I reached over and took hold of the hand of the very clean, very neat, immaculate girl who had said "dirty and filthy."

"I wouldn't believe it. Nobody would do a thing like that."

"I would feel all good inside. Someone cared very much about me."

Of course, I found it impossible to convey the full import of Jesus' act. The biblical diagnosis of leprosy is different from today's understanding of leprosy. The issue then, according to the law, was ritual uncleanness rather than contagion. The great Jewish scholar Claude Montefiore has asserted that that act of touching the unclean leper marked *the* new note in the ministry of Jesus. It cut through all the legal qualifications of the Jewish law and tore down all the human barriers to genuine acceptance: "Here was a new and lofty note, a new and exquisite manifestation of the very pity and love which the prophets had demanded." [1]

Even though my church school youngsters could not experience that "new" and "exquisite" move, they did begin to sense the power present when a person who regards himself as bad is physically touched by a person who is esteemed as good.

When I removed my hand, the fastidious girl brushed the hand that I had held with her other hand, as though to brush away my touch.

"You didn't like my touching you," I commented.

"Oh, no!" She laughed uneasily and then reached out and put her hand on my arm, saying, "I was only kidding. I didn't mind."

THE TOUCH TABOO

She *did* mind; yet she was "touched." The next Sunday our relationship had moved to another level. No longer was there the impassive, controlled caution which had characterized our interactions. When we saw each other, her face broke out in a warm and sparkling smile. We had something going between us. We had made contact. Somehow my touch—and her touch—had sparked our relationship to life. And I felt good all over.

In that girl's ambivalence lies some of our human hangup, especially of white middle-class Americans. Spirit is split off from body. We live imprisoned behind an invisible shield—the touch taboo. To pass through that protective covering constitutes the last stage in reducing the distance between oneself and another.

Psychologist Sidney Jourard [2] watched pairs of people talking with each other in various places. He counted the number of times one person touched the other person in the course of an hour. The scores are revealing:

San Juan, Puerto Rico	180
Paris	110
London	0
Gainesville, Florida	2

Similarly, in a two-hour observation in the Teaching Hospital at the University of Florida, he watched the interaction between nurses, physicians, patients, and relatives. During that period "two nurses' hands touched those of the patients to whom they were giving pills; one physician held a patient's wrist as he was taking a pulse; and one intern placed his arm around the waist of a student nurse to whom he was engaged." [3]

On the basis of his exploratory study of body contact, Jourard proposed that "only those persons who have a relationship with others that includes touching and caressing will have a fully experienced body and a fully embodied self." [4]

We are cut off from ourselves, from each other, from meaning. We long to be in contact with ourselves, with each other, with meaning. Yet a means to meaning—human contact, physical touch—makes us uncomfortable even as we hunger for the comfort which contact can bring.

Rebirth in the Spirit and recovery of the body go hand-in-hand. Without our physical base we have no spiritual reality. Without spiritual vitality we have no physical reality. "The Word became flesh"—*sarx,* flesh and blood, a human being, bodied existence (which is the only existence possible). To be in touch with reality is linked with being in touch as "flesh." To be touched is to come alive!

THE HUNGER FOR CONTACT

As parents, we had cuddled and held and hugged our children. We had reached out for contact because we had wanted to. When Ronald was with us, we learned the necessity of physical contact. Part of his strange gait and awkward motions came from stimulus deprivation. He had not been held and cuddled and hugged. That lack of physical contact retarded the maturation of his neuromuscular equipment. We were advised to touch him and stroke him and hold him as much as possible.

Physical contact constitutes the initial language of life and the primary language of love.

I especially remember one moment during my own experience of psychotherapy. A total letting go had occurred. It came at the end of a very trying session. With deep feeling, I had voiced many hurts and much anger. As I got up to leave, I sank back on the couch and went to pieces—sobbing and sobbing and sobbing. At that moment my intellectualizing was gone. Specific content was absent. There was nothing but raw emotion.

My therapist was a reserved person by temperament. But at that moment he came over, put his arm around my shoulders, and was simply "with" me in a way that was uncharacteristic of him. We said nothing, for there was nothing to be said. We only let the moment "be" what it was. We "stayed with" what was happening until it had passed.

I would have pulled myself together within a few minutes whether or not he had come near. Even though my defenses were down, I was not coming apart at the seams. My progress in therapy would have continued acceptably without that gesture on his part. Yet, in my letting go and in his holding on, I was beginning (to use Fritz Perls' dictum) to lose my "mind" and come to my *senses.*[5]

Although consciousness is the defining attribute of human beings, consciousness can constrict into narrow intellectualism. Those who have had the privilege of extensive education run the danger of thinking more and more while feeling less and less. They achieve a mind but lose a body. The source of spontaneity, inspiration, intuition, and vitality dries up. The result is that they shrink into pale and lifeless caricatures of what they might have been.

During the last fifteen years the revolt against sterile intellectualism has gathered momentum. The cry for human warmth has been raised within the realm of the religious as well as within the field of psychology. Surprising as the thought may be, I believe the "soul" and Pentecostal movements in the churches and the sensitivity movement in psychology are similar responses to human starvation. Let's look closely at these two movements.

The Sensitivity Movement in Psychology

Following upon the relatively impersonal quality of early Freudian analysis, we find increasingly a new personal emphasis. The labels differ but the realities overlap:

presence,
participation,
encounter,
confrontation,
mutuality,
wholeness.

The development of sensitivity training, group laboratories, and human relations workshops since World War II may prove, in retrospect, to be the single most significant advance in the psychological field during this period. "Human" contact and human "becoming" combine the means and the end.

One account may be enough to suggest the means-end of sensitivity experiences.

In describing various techniques for expanding human awareness, William Schutz reports one woman's fantasy voyage into her inner space. To begin, she was asked to make herself small and to enter her body whenever she was ready. She was to go to that part of her body about which she had the most conflict. Here are excerpts from her own description:

> Suddenly, I saw my heart. It was floating in my chest cavity with no attachments—just suspended in nothingness. I was very *frightened by the detachment.* . .
>
> "Can you get across to it?" Bill asked.
> "No! It's too smooth and slippery." . .
> (Can you build a bridge?)
> "I can try. I'll put a plank across." . . . I . . . started gingerly across.
>
> Suddenly, the plank began to buckle up and down. "It's an earthquake!"
> (Can you get some help?)
> "Yes. I'll call out the Earthquake Rescue Squad." . . .
> (Can you make the bridge more secure?) . . . (Can you get someone to help you?)
>
> Suddenly, the Jolly Green Giant . . . offered, "How would you like a can of peas for a heart?" . . . "No, thanks," I told him, *"I want a human heart."* [6]

And so her journey unfolded. Schutz assumed that it was his job to aid her to integrate her heart with the rest of her being. Her difficulties centered on managing her feelings of affection. "If she could build sound bridges from her heart to the rest of her body perhaps her love feelings could be handled more realistically in relation to herself." While her struggle with loving and being loved continued, she grew more able to cope satisfactorily with her life.[7]

People are being brought back to their senses by means of sensory awakening.[8] In the sensitivity movement the recovery of the human heart explicitly draws upon religious means and meaning. The following excerpts from the most widely known book of experiments in being alive disclose that connection:

Touch
has always been
a most effective method
of healing. The energy
that flows through the hands
can refresh, regenerate,
revitalize.
The laying on of hands
can create great
physical-mental changes.
In the hands of a person
who understands, touch
sometimes can be as effective
as drugs or surgery.

Worship: contact
with the ground of being:
A part not apart of existence.
Pouring the wine
need not be anybody's blood;
it's divine by its very substance.
Fill your cup, feel
its weight, taste its flavor,
pass it to,
see your neighbor.

The breaking of bread,
not anyone's flesh,
the miracle is
right before your eyes,
ears, nose, mouth.
Forget the abstractions
and chew, true communion:
love sacred, sharing contact,
caring for yourself,
for others.

The washing of feet,
the laying on of hands
relaxation and
other sensory experiences can
help bring ritual,
religion back to life.[9]

The words sound religious, but they come from sensitivity experiences.

The Spirit Movement in Religion

There is a relatively controlled quality in formalized Christianity. It has developed partially because people have feared their emotions and partially because people have desired to organize their collective experience. Nevertheless, we find increasingly a new emphasis. The labels differ; the realities overlap:

Spirit,

celebration,

soul,

festivity,

transcendence,

ecstasy,

underground.

The search for new life in the Spirit permeates religious consciousness.

At the turn of the century, W. E. B. Du Bois voiced the passionate unfolding of the blacks' bitter struggle for human rights. Two-thirds of a century later, theologian James Cone sharpened the tie between *human rights* and *human religion* when he declared: "To be for God by responding creatively to the *imago Dei* means that man cannot allow others to make him an It. It is this fact that makes black rebellion human and religious." [10] But it was still Du Bois who wrote of the soul hunger, "the restlessness of the savage, the wail of the wanderer, and the plaint is put in one little phrase":

My soul wants some - thing that's new, that's new [11]

One account may be enough to suggest the end-means of the spiritual vitality phenomenon. Reporter John Sherrill, an upper middle-class Episcopalian, set out to investigate the Pentecostal movement as a result of a combination of an intense personal crisis and an unexpected comment in a regular editorial meeting. From an initial stance of scientific objectivity, Sherrill eventually found himself a renewed Christian. Along the way he "felt like a man who had stooped to pet a kitten and finds his hand on a tiger." [12]

Behind the religious expression we find personal experience. Without negating the attributed source of the Spirit to God, we can see human contact as a means of meaning and the loss of sterile rationality as a recovery of vitality. Speaking in tongues and touching go together. Spiritual emotion and physical motion are linked.

Sherrill tells of his own resistance to one act which many Pentecostals perform: standing up, raising both hands toward heaven, and shouting, "Praise the Lord!" In his experience of breakthrough, he tells of being in a hotel room at a Pentecostal convention with five non-Pentecostals who had begun to find new life in the Spirit.

> Someone began to pray. . . . Minds seemed to work together. . . .
>
> Now someone else began to pray in tongues. Another started to sing very softly in the Spirit. I felt my throat tighten. . . . I suppose I was crying, deeply, silently. Slowly I began to lose my own identity too, until finally self-awareness disappeared.
>
> . . . the very nature of that hour was pure experience, with a maximum of *allowing to happen what was going to happen,* and a minimum of analysis.
>
> The group moved closer around me. It was almost as if they were *forming with their bodies* a funnel through which was concentrated the flow of the Spirit that was pulsing through that room.
>
> And suddenly I had the impression that in order to speak in tongues I had only to look up. But this was a joyful gesture. All my training and inclination was to approach God with head bowed.
>
> . . . Strange that *such a simple gesture as lifting the head* should become a battleground. . . . not only was I to lift my head but I was to *lift my hands too,* and I was *to cry out* with all the feeling in me a great shout of praise to God. A hot, angry flush rose and flooded me. It was the thing above all things that I didn't want to do.
>
> With a sudden burst of will *I thrust my hands into the air, turned my face full upward,* and at the top of my voice *I shouted:*
> "Praise the Lord!"
> It was the floodgate opened. From deep inside me, deeper than I knew voice could go, came a torrent of joyful sound. . . . It was healing, it was forgiveness, it was love too deep for words and it burst from me in wordless sound. After that one shattering effort of will, *my will was released.* . . . No further conscious effort was required of me at all, not even choosing the syllables with which to express my joy.
>
> It was not that I felt out of control of the situation: I had never felt more *truly master of myself,* more integrated and at peace with warring factions inside myself. . . . I prayed on, laughing and free. I, self-centered, introverted, preoccupied with my own problems, suddenly found myself going out of my way to know other people, really caring about them, really wanting to help. And as soon as anyone does that, of course, the possibilities of being used are endless.[13]

Sensitivity movement people will undoubtedly be uncomfortable by my linking them with the kind of spiritual experience described by Sherrill. Spirit movement people will unquestionably be disturbed by my associating them with the kind of sensitivity experience described by Schutz. Yet within each I find.

> recovery of the body
> > recovery of human contact
> > > recovery of life's possibilities
>
> losing one's mind
> coming to one's senses.

RECOVERY OF THE BODY

The body as the base of the person has reemerged. From having been experienced as "base-bad" the body may once again be known as "base-solid." In a real sense it is our human alpha and omega, our human beginning and end.

The body talks. Its language may be subtle or blunt. Words may express or confuse the basic body message. But behind, within, and beyond what we say we come upon what we *body*.

One woman with whom I had been working referred to "body talk." In the midst of recording our conversations she remarked, "I think it would be nice if that tape could hear your nodding head and nice smile—just kind of encouraging, the way your face talks to me. I've learned a lot about 'body talk' from you."

Since then, I have learned that research has established a formula that gives more precision to this woman's observation. Words, voice, and face in combination produce the effect of any message as a whole. The formula reads:

"Total Impact $= .07$ verbal $+ .38$ vocal $+ .55$ facial." [14]

Words themselves actually make slight impact. At a subliminal level we listen more to the vocal quality—the tone, the intonation, the stress, the length and frequency of pauses, and so on. At the visual level we listen mostly to the facial expression, gestures, movements, and body position. What we *see* turns out to be the most powerful communicator of what is said.

Body talk emphasizes the physical dimension of the person as the active component in interpersonal communication. Body talk may be a nodding head, a frozen smile, a puzzled frown, or an inviting gesture. It may be the way one sits, the way one shifts position, the way one gets up, or the way one walks. The figurative use of body language underscores the point:

shoulder a burden	get it off your chest
chin up	get off my back
pain in the neck	no backbone
hard-nosed	my aching back
can't stomach it	stand on your own feet
broken-hearted	knuckle under.[15]

Body and spirit reflect and reinforce each other.

Not only does the body talk in terms of what we see and sense but the body also talks in terms of direct contact. It is the literal touch that I want to examine as crucial in the process of personal change.

For several months I had been seeing a college junior in counseling sessions once every week. During the whole period she agonized over talking with me about anything. In the middle of one session she came to a complete stop and left. In the next session she again reached a dead end. She felt that there was nothing more to do. We were getting nowhere. She did agree, however, to return one more time.

Within the first five minutes in that "final" session she again blocked. In working with the block—getting her to fantasize how she experienced the obstacle and then to visualize it—I figured out what was between us and told her. She gasped for breath as though I had hit her in the stomach. By the end of the session she agreed to continue to see me and made an appointment for her regular time a week later.

For her, the days that followed swelled with stress. She could not eat. She did not do well on perceptual tasks in her psychology course. Finally, in desperation, she called and asked for a special appointment. Several weeks later, she tried to reflect on what had helped her in that special session, for it had marked a turning point in her growth as a person:

"I don't know," she mused. "I didn't—I know I didn't say very much. I just—was upset, felt a little foolish for coming. I mean, I shook all the way here. My mouth was just so dry I could hardly talk. And I—I tried to talk. And you kept asking me, 'Well, do you want to talk about it?' or 'Well, can you say you don't want to talk about it?' And I was trying so hard to be so reasonable—trying to reason everything out."

With this statement she clearly illustrated Fritz Perls' point. In her desperate struggle to keep her head she had lost touch with her feelings. She believed that if she let go, she would lose control, and to lose control was to fall apart. In contrast, I was proceeding on the assumption that if she could let go, she would come together. Her forgetting her reasoning would enable her to recover her experiencing.

She continued her reflection: "You said, 'Do you want to cry?' And I said, 'Yes! But I can't.' And you said, 'Can you say you don't want to cry?' And I (laughing a little) said, 'Well, I *do* want to cry.' 'Well, can you say that you don't?' I said it. And you said, 'Say it again.' And I did. And you said, 'Again.'

"And I almost did (spoken with more life). I was almost crying. And you got up and came over and sat beside me. You took my hands—And I just completely broke. I—no one's ever seen me like that before, so completely—I—I had no idea what I was saying. I just sort of poured out how discouraged I was—And I *appreciated* that because I think if you hadn't come over to me, I think I'd have tried to pull everything back into me."

"In other words," I asked, "physically reaching out helped you to come out?"

"Yes, yes, it did," she affirmed. "I mean, I was just sitting there like this, just trying to pull everything into me." With that she proceeded to cross her arms very tightly across her chest, hunch her shoulders over, and press her legs very tightly together and against the chair. "And," she continued, "if you had stayed on the other side of the room, you would have been there but, I—I wouldn't have been so aware of it or that you— that you—cared!"

"What made it possible to accept this?" I wondered. "Because, you know, any physical contact for you is so uncomfortable."

"I know it," she responded. For she was touchy about being touched. "I don't know what it was. I—it was—it was just at that moment I was so in need of someone to hang on to, to actually hang on to—and I never had before—I never had actually felt the need to—to hang on. I'd always been pretty much self-sufficient," she explained, "holding other people off at arm's length. And I—I couldn't. I needed so much not to be cut off—And, well, it's the first time I ever called you by your first name, too." She spoke with deep pleasure at the memory of the breakthrough.

"You weren't thinking," I pointed out, trying to reinforce the way in which she used her mind to ward off her spontaneity.

"It's easier," she went on, "to hold you off if I call you 'Mister,' too. I keep you on the other side of the room. I wasn't thinking," she concurred. "It just came out. I don't know why. It was just that I felt so much better when I left. It was as though I didn't have to push back what was bothering me any more. It would stay there until our next appointment. I noticed it was more manageable after having talked about it, after having remembered I was so terribly upset. It meant if I hadn't come, I would have disciplined myself to work, and I would have had an awful time bringing it up the next week. I can't know what would have happened, actually."

She sat quietly for a long time. I experienced nothing of the blocking and resisting of previous pauses. This time she was simply living in the moment. Then she went on.

"I don't know why I've been able to talk to you like this. I just feel that I can. Now all of a sudden there are a lot of things in the open that should have been in the open a long time ago."

It takes little insight to realize what a withdrawn and tied-up person she was. In intimate encounter her longing for contact and her fear of contact paralyzed her. Even in casual brushes with people she moved only with great exertion of will power.

The shock of recognition of what was blocking her communication with me precipitated a crisis. Either she had to move into her anxiety or flee back into work. To have knuckled down more in her studies would have meant more knuckling under to her neurosis. She said with her words that she wanted to break through and make contact, but she spoke with her body to the contrary. Her accumulated reserve and imagined self-sufficiency acted to hold her back. My going to her, reaching out, and taking her hands so that she could "actually" hang on gave her the necessary courage to let down her defenses. By hanging on, she could let go. She interpreted my physical gesture as a sign that I "cared."

Another girl, twenty-two years of age and married, presented a somewhat different pattern. Her parents had separated when she was five. As a result of continuing to live with her mother, she had had no contact with or word about her father in the years since. In the course of our counseling together the following picture emerged: an underlying dissatisfaction with life, an unhealthy marriage, a feeling of emptiness about religion. She appeared to be strong and resourceful; she was, in fact, dependent and fearful.

At the end of an interview in which the full weight of her life situation erupted into awareness, she fell apart. The defenses she had used to protect her sense of self collapsed. Instead of release and relief there came only chaotic turbulence. All of the hurts, resentments, disappointments, frustrations, and expectations that had been denied poured in. Her body ached. Her mind spun. She experienced panic.

For a period of ten days her panic ebbed and flowed. One moment she would be drowning in the flood of emotion; the next she would lie exhausted from the intensity of the experience. She withdrew from activity and people. She contemplated suicide as the only way out. She talked of wanting to push everything and everyone away.

I felt that, if she also wanted to push me away, steps should be taken immediately to hospitalize her. I was her one link with life. If even that link was gone, she was lost.

I asked her if she could push me away. To make the reality concrete, I put out my hands, palms facing her, for her to push me away. She made a feeble attempt and then sank back into the chair saying she could not do it. On the basis of that response, the decision was made (with a psychiatric consultant) to continue the risk of allowing her to stay in the community. We believed that to hospitalize her would prematurely resolve the panic. She might have to go through an even more traumatic experience in the future unless she assimilated then what she had denied for so long.

After the panic had passed, she went back over the experience in our conversation as a way of taking in and making her own what had happened.

"I felt a responsibility toward you," she told me. "I mean, you made me feel the responsibility toward myself; let's put it that way. You being there and your spending time with me and being interested made me feel like—well, everything couldn't be lost, you know."

"Because I cared," I interpreted, "you cared."

"Yeh—it helped a great deal just to know, those couple of weeks there, that you were geographically close."

Then she picked up another thread of association. "And another thing that's been helpful: Many times I would keep coming back, even though many times it would be very, very painful, because you would sum up what I'd been saying or say things to me which were truths about myself which I didn't want to face. But I knew you were only trying to help me to think them through. It's been very hard for me ever to find anyone who was objective and at the same time—ah, didn't criticize. The objectivity with which you could help me look at myself helped me. I also felt that you were a sympathetic person who was helping me to live through this. And this made me keep coming back, even though it hurt."

She tried to distinguish what I had done from *what she had done.*

"One of the big things that I think has really been good about this experience," she continued, "is the way you've handled it in never putting pressure on me to come back. You were always saying, well, if I want to do it. That has made me feel that no matter how much I felt like I wanted to lean on you that in coming out of this experience I have done this on my own."

"In other words," I reflected, "I haven't taken over responsibility for you?"

"Yes. You have made me feel that if I have lived, I have wanted to. I have kept the decision to keep on living, even though I did say I felt this responsibility toward you, but still it was my decision. And it was my own decision to keep on coming back. I did it because I wanted to help myself. This— this—is a wonderful feeling to feel like it's—it's—you're doing something on your own. And yet, somebody is there helping you and you are able to accept the help you get."

"You did it on your own," I summarized, "but you weren't alone."

"*Yeh,* yeh," she was almost chanting. "That's right! That's right!" She had found a way between the necessary independence on the one side and the necessary dependence on the other. She had been on her own yet not alone.

But the path had not been as neat and easy as our conversation

implies. The physical interaction that encouraged us not to
hospitalize her had created an unanticipated complication.

"I was trying so hard to find something I could be close to,"
she explained, "to hold on to. I couldn't push you away when
you asked me to. I mean, it was just like a nightmare. And it
makes me hurt even now."

I could see her hurt, but I wanted to understand its cause
more clearly: "In other words, you needed to hang on to me
at that point?"

"And not push you away," she hastened to add. "You were
trying to make me push you away and I couldn't." She sat very
still and seemed to be thinking deeply. After a long pause, she
added, "It took me a long time to get over that. And sometimes
. . . when I'm half awake and half dreaming I—I think of that
and it really hurts!"

Her hurt was coming across loud and clear. The desirable
act had let loose an undesirable reaction. Since it had been
physical contact that had set up the pain, it seemed that only
physical contact could undo the pain.

"Can you draw me close?"

"What do you mean?"

"Well," I explained, "if your hurt comes from pushing me
away and you are still hurting, we might reverse the experience
now. That is, can you pull me close to you?"

We both got out of our chairs. She gripped me tightly around
the waist, squeezing as if to make certain I was there. She was
breathing heavily, letting out gasps every now and then. Between
sobs she told me, "This physical contact has helped, too.
It's so good to know there is somebody—somebody to put his arm
around me or hold my hand and feel that."

We sat down; she continued to describe what physical contact
meant to her. "People are so awkward about that," she
observed, "even my mother and family. I remember that day
I went up to your house during the panic. Your wife gave me a
nightgown while I slept there. And she just held out her arms
to me and, and, I just hugged her for a minute. I needed that
so much."

Here again we sense the desperate need of one person to hold
on to another person in a very literal sense. It indicates severe
emotional deprivation of a primary sort. Words cannot carry

the burden of the personal relationship. Physical contact is required.

Similar demands are present in terms of aggression and hostility. Where the desire to strangle a certain individual became so intense that no words could express it, I had one person grab hold of my arm and squeeze as hard as he could. In another counseling situation I had someone hit my open palm as though he were smashing the face of the person he resented so deeply. In still another situation a woman took sheets of paper and ripped them up as though she were tearing to pieces the target of her hostility.

Since we are acting organisms and not merely talking organisms, contact with the reality of our experience requires physical expression. Without this, that which comes into awareness is blunted. Full ambivalence is paralyzed. A resolution of the polarity between love and hate is compromised, reinforcing withdrawal and continued repression.

RECOVERY OF HUMAN CONTACT

What I am saying is that we are physical creatures.

As the apostle Paul insisted, the only human existence possible, even in the realm of the Spirit, is somatic existence. *Soma,* or body, belongs to the very essence of the self. I *am soma.* It is incorrect to say that I *have* a *soma.* It is not that we have a body but that we *are* body. *"Man is called soma in respect to his being able to make himself the object of his own action,"* writes Rudolf Bultmann, *"or to experience himself as the subject to whom something happens . . . as having a relationship to himself."* [16] Therefore, we can be at one with ourselves or at odds with ourselves.

"Insofar as man is *soma* and thereby has a relationship to himself, he can distinguish himself from himself, and he will do this all the more as he experiences outside powers trying to wrest him out of his own control or even having done so." [17] Even as we are ashamed of our aggressive feelings, so we are embarrassed by our affectionate feelings. We keep our heads, for fear of losing our bodies. What occurs, in fact, is that in keeping our heads we lose our lives. Our emotions act as though they were guerrillas sabotaging our reason. Our minds turn into unreliable guides distorting our feelings. The creative depths of personal life and personal relationships are lost.

The early church provides a significant example of this. Jesus gave his disciples a new commandment: "By this all men will know that you are my disciples, if you have love [*agape*] for one another." The First Letter of John adds: "We have passed out of death into life, because we love [*agape*]. . . ." [18]

In the light of this background we can understand a custom that grew up in the life of the early church. The apostle Paul speaks of it in several letters.[19] By the time of Justin Martyr in A.D. 150, it had become a fixed part of worship, a liturgical greeting which symbolized Christian brotherhood. This is the way in which Paul puts it: "Greet one another with a holy kiss." The First Letter of Peter gives a slightly different version: "Greet one another with the kiss of love." J. B. Phillips, in his modern translation of these passages, alters the wording to fit white middle-class reserve: "Give one another a handshake all round as a sign of love."

Love—*agape*—is elevated as the mark of genuine community. This love is not disembodied thought or detached words. It is an outgoing, spontaneous, warm, caring, affectionate, nonpossessive, unconditional, nonlustful concern for another. It activates the whole person. It embraces man as physical organism because apart from our bodies we do not exist.

One woman in client-centered therapy describes this same kind of love independent of the biblical and theological roots to which I have just referred:

> It's a different kind of—sexual feeling . . . it's one that is stripped of all the—the things that have happened to sex. . . . There's no—chase, no pursuit, no—battle, no—well, no kind of hate, which I think . . . has crept into such things. . . .
> [It's a] kind of radiant warmth which completely restores. . . . It's . . . a type of love, for which there is no personal gratification.[20]

The early church called the kiss "holy," "sacred," "sanctifying" because it represented the peace which is only created by genuine affection. The kiss served as the tangible expression of the inward ties of human relationship.

The practice of the holy kiss continued in the church for many years. Eventually, it had to be abandoned, for it came to be abused. I suppose some of the brethren took the act to mean lustful sex rather than genuine affection. The men probably used it as an excuse to paw the women, while some of the women undoubtedly used it as an excuse to be pawed. In either case the act became exploitative. It degenerated into physiological gratification, not personal sharing.

To raise the issue of physical contact in counseling, as well as in everyday relationships, is to touch upon a potentially explosive area.

When I used the account of the young married woman's panic in a semipopular professional journal article, the editor expressed apprehension "about the danger of encouraging male ministers who are amateurs in pastoral counseling . . . to 'hug' their female parishioners when they come to them for help. I am fully aware of your own awareness of this danger," he wrote, "which you so vividly warn against . . . but I have known of psychiatrists and psychoanalysts who have gone to bed with their patients and rationalized it as being therapeutic, and I just dread the possibility of this very important aspect of a relationship being misinterpreted and misapplied—again, in spite of your vivid warning." To meet his concern, I deleted the section describing reversing the woman's hurt at pushing me away by pulling me close. Even so, the editor prefaced the article with a long introductory note admitting to hesitation about its publication and concern about "the possible misuse that could be made of the 'physical.' "

The editor's concern is not unwarranted. With the mushrooming of the new industry of human growth, warnings have matched claims as to the value of sensitivity. However, the fact that bodied existence constitutes a problem is no reason to reject the body. It is our *human* loss that as we attempt to control the fires of life we easily extinguish them altogether. In so doing, we diminish the creative possibilities within us and among us.

I suggest that we need to rediscover the inner dynamics and meaning of the holy kiss—simple physical contact—the touch of person with person that is appropriate in the immediate situation. Usually this is most commonly experienced and expressed at funerals and weddings. We place a hand on the arm; we plant a kiss on the cheek; we embrace spontaneously. In such acts we say more adequately what we can say only inadequately with words. The power of physical personal contact cannot be overestimated. Neither must it be underestimated.

In describing the maturing of the group encounter phenomenon, Carl Rogers speaks of the closer and more direct contact people have with each other in groups than in ordinary life. He reports the experience of a mother with several children who speaks of herself as " 'a loud, prickly, hyperactive individual' whose marriage was on the rocks" and for whom life was not worth living. After the group encounter she wrote to another participant telling what had happened to her:

> The real turning point for me was a simple gesture on your part of putting your arm around my shoulder one afternoon after I had made some crack about the fact that no one could cry on your shoulder. In my notes I had written the night before, "there is no man in the world who loves me." You seemed so genuinely concerned that day that I was overwhelmed. I *received* the gesture as one of the first feelings of acceptance of *me*—just the dumb way I am, prickles and all—that I have ever experienced. I have felt needed, loving, competent, furious, frantic, everything and anything but just plain *loved*. You can imagine the flood of gratitude, humility and release that swept over me. I write with considerable joy, *"I actually felt loved."* [21]

I have linked the sensitivity movement in psychology with the spirit emphasis in religion. The connection, I believe, lies in the power of such human contact as that mother expressed. It is this which is causing American churches to turn to sensitivity procedures. "Experiential" worship stresses not only the nonverbal and multimedia but, even more, it stresses worship by physical contact.

One of the most controversial events on the fringes of the Fourth Assembly of the World Council of Churches meeting in Uppsala, Sweden, in the summer of 1968, was an experiment in experiential worship. A special report to *The New York Times* describes some of the ways used to increase physical contact and communication between worshipers:

> Standing with her eyes closed and her feet close together, a young woman allowed her limp body to be passed slowly from hand to hand by four men standing in a small circle.
>
> "The purpose is to see how much we are willing to trust ourselves and each other," said the leader.
>
> Then each of the five participants walked up to the others one at a time, touched them on the hands or shoulders and told them "what I like most about you."
>
> "You have such a warm smile," said the woman to a youth.
>
> "I appreciate your being so open," said an older man to another. [22]

Both the exercise in falling and the exercise in touching and telling were part of a larger attempt to experience the reality of each other and the reality of God.

I am not suggesting that pastors and counselors begin indiscriminately to touch or hug or kiss their parishioners and counselees. That could be damaging, especially because even the counselors tend to be uncomfortable with their genuine feelings of affection. But I am convinced that the power of the personal lies within the meaning of physical contact.

The complexity of such pastoral relationships was best expressed by another woman with whom I worked in a therapeutic process. She had read an article of mine on the lost dimension of the physical and wanted me to know her reaction, "particularly," she wrote, "in light of the way I felt in our counseling sessions—both when you didn't touch me and the way I felt when you finally did. I find I both agree and disagree with your warnings. I think you are partially right that a physical expression could be misunderstood—as it surely would have been by me in our earlier sessions. And yet it was also the lack of such which I felt blocked our relationship and only when you finally did 'touch' me, did I really feel accepted.

"To me," she concluded forcefully, "the fact that you wouldn't touch me meant that you could not accept my sickness at that point—which was so tied up with the need for contact and physical acceptance."

How can the distorted be distinguished from the healing in human contact? I suspect that there are no easy answers.

Obviously, if I am not finding a satisfying and fulfilling intimacy outside the pastoral or counseling relationship, I am more susceptible to misusing the powerful tool of contact. Obviously, I need to be sensitive to what holding out my hand or putting my arm around a shoulder might mean to the other person. Obviously, if I am uncertain of what is going on between myself and another, it is wise for me to maintain a respectful distance. Obviously, what is meant to be a deeply personal and genuinely spontaneous act may deteriorate into a mere technique or a mechanical ritual designed to manipulate the other. Only as motion and emotion are congruent does the Word become flesh.

It is my hunch that the greatest power of contact comes primarily in moments of deep agony or great ecstasy. Both of these are turning points. In the agony we come upon unsuspected courage enabling us to pierce through every negativity and find underneath the everlasting arms. In the ecstasy we enter into ecstasy's fullness by being carried beyond ourselves into a larger communion. Shared agony and shared ecstasy are shared most fully by means of human contact.

The significance of the recovery of human contact by the recovery of body talk came home with sharp impact one day when I was calling on an eighty-three-year-old parishioner. For two and one-half years she had been bedfast with terminal cancer. During that time I had called on her about every other month. She was a demanding person. Neither I nor others could ever show her enough attention. Her very complaining conditioned people to avoid her. I, too, was so conditioned, I am chagrined to confess.

On that particular day, as we talked, I felt a wave of deep and genuine affection flow through me. For the first time I responded to her personally and warmly. I felt alive and good because I was with her. After reading a passage of Scripture and praying, I rose to leave. This time I bent over and kissed her on the cheek.

A look of astonishment crossed her face. After a stunned moment, she said, "Why, I'm not ugly after all. I'm not ugly after all."

The holy kiss—or whatever the expression of human contact might be—is the outward and tangible sign of inward acceptance. When we let go of our self-consciousness, we do find life together!

Four

Agony and Ecstasy
in the Parish Context

How fragile and fleeting is our recovery of human contact!

In a moment of anxiety the comfort of human contact evaporates. In a move to another city it breaks apart. In the relentless bulldozing of time its inspiration fades. And again we experience ourselves as Giacometti's tall, tightly stretched figures: eroded by nature, stripped of sophistication, isolated, and lonely.

PARISH STRENGTHS

For a pastor to reach out to touch the person of another may be a gesture necessary for the recovery of human contact. Yet his gesture alone can seldom, if ever, be sufficient for full human presence. More is needed. That *more* is a context; it is a place where presence is given and presence is received; it is a place where people are *with* and *for* each other.

The Subtlety of Context

In their empirical study of the meaning of context, Seward Hiltner and Lowell Colston, in my judgment, focused on the crucial variable in pastoral counseling.

They rightly assumed that what goes on between a pastor and a parishioner is the same as what goes on between a psychotherapist and a client. Regardless of professional training, the helping process includes acceptance, understanding, and clarification of inner conflicts. These come as a consequence of creating and maintaining a sense of trust between the one seeking help and the one giving help.[1]

In that sense pastoral counseling is still counseling. At the same time, however, the helping relationship is always carried out by different individuals wearing different professional hats. The authors contended (and I concur) that the hat a person wears—the context in which he works, the role he carries—sharpens his uniqueness and decisively influences his distinctiveness in relation to other helping persons. They postulated four dimensions to the meaning of context: setting, expectation, the shift in relationship, and aims and limitations.

1. The setting symbolizes to the person seeking help everything for which the church stands. His views may be positive, negative, or mixed. "Church" has different meanings for different persons.
2. These meanings are expressed in the expectations which people bring to their relationship with the pastor as minister.
3. To be sure, the person seeks out the pastor with a general idea of what he expects of ministers, but he comes with also a more specific idea in mind. It is that specific intent that indicates the shift in the relationship. Previously, there had been an informal give-and-take between them; now there is a more focused encounter. The person wants a closer relationship that is both helping and temporary.
4. In terms of aims for what they are about and limitations in what they undertake, the pastor's concern tends to be all encompassing. His specific aim is to assist the person to deal with his immediate and limited crisis. By so doing, he hopes to reawaken the deeper meanings of the person's life.[2]

Hiltner and Colston concluded that "the attempt to understand and to articulate . . . the feelings people have about the whole context in which pastoral counseling takes place, is not a nuisance but a vital instrument in the giving of help.[3]

For the purposes of their research, Colston served as a minister who specialized in counseling in a church of 2500 members. Thus he was part of the ministerial staff. The context and role definition sharpened the distinction between the pastor counselor and the psychological counselor, at least as carried on by Colston in his role at the church and in a similar though different role at the University of Chicago Counseling Center where he was known as a psychologist.

The Counseling Pastor

A further distinction is desirable. The *pastoral* counselor and the counseling *pastor* play different roles. The pastoral counselor is a specialist. He is usually part of a team. Whereas his work may take place in the context of the parish, and although the pastoral image helps to sharpen his own and others' expectations, his relationship with the person seeking help tends to be more limited, as is the case with other helping professionals.

In contrast, the counseling pastor, who carries the chief responsibility for the total congregational life, has a more extensive and varied pattern of relationships with the person seeking help. Seldom is the person meeting the pastor for the first time, nor will their sessions in the counseling chamber be the last time they see each other. The counseling relationship with a pastor is usually a special one. It is helping, temporary, and derived from a more general matrix of interaction.

In a period when the pressure for specialization, of which *pastoral* counseling is an inevitable, necessary, and legitimate expression, the pastor as a generalist feels increasingly handicapped and anachronistic. The pastor who counsels as part of his overall parish responsibility wonders about his place in the field of counseling. Feeling that he has nothing distinctive to contribute, he sees only his liabilities and his limitations. He tends to lack the confidence that accompanies specialized skill. He misses the protection of a carefully structured formal procedure. In short, as a helping person he feels second-rate and out of place.

It is my conviction that the reverse is closer to the truth of the situation. Instead of being a drawback, the parish is the asset *par excellence* in counseling. By virtue of his parish context, the pastor finds himself in a distinct situation with distinct possibilities for the helping process.

I do not mean to reduce the importance of the role of the specialist. I myself am a specialist of sorts. Rather, I want to activate the role of the generalist.

Specialization in counseling provides more sophisticated approaches, especially in intervening in character disorder patterns and in focusing upon changing behavior as a way of modifying feelings as much as changing feelings through insight as a way of modifying behavior.

The generalist, however, provides a more complete model of presence—being for others—by virtue of the greater complexity of situational variables.

In order to be more specific in the implications of my conviction about the primacy of the parish as the context of helping, let me describe a counseling relationship which I had in one of the parishes where I served as minister. Using the transcript of a discussion in which a parishioner looks back upon the counseling relationship, I want to explore within a parish context the counseling process as conducted by a minister who primarily carried responsibility for the total local church. From the transcript several characteristics of the counseling *pastor* and his functioning emerge.

The Situation

Before turning to the transcript, however, some background will be helpful. Both the husband and the wife took part in church life. They attended regularly, participated in activities, and held positions in the organizational structure. To the casual observer everything seemed fine.

The wife, a woman in her mid-forties, had told me that things were not well in their marriage. They had visited a psychiatrist at her insistence, but the husband felt no need for help. I suggested that if anything were to change, she herself would probably have to be the one to change. I made that suggestion in a special call to their apartment for that purpose. That act of going out of my way to talk with her about the family meant a great deal to her. Clearly, anyone who struggles with low self-esteem and high anxiety finds such initiative supportive.

Subsequently, she came to me with a specific desire to enter into an extended counseling relationship. We met once a week for twenty-one weeks. Nine months after we had stopped, we met again for two additional sessions. One year later the interview occurred from which the material for the rest of this chapter is drawn. I had asked her if she would be willing to reflect on what had happened in order to help parish ministers understand some of the possibilities and difficulties of counseling parishioners.

I am using the case as a way of suggesting and illustrating aspects of the place of the gesture that are particularly applicable to counseling by the pastor. Its value, I believe, lies more in that toward which it points than in that which it demonstrates. I never regarded myself as understanding the woman and her family situation in the sense of "standing under" what was happening. I never found therapeutic techniques that seemed to help, even though I had continual supervision by a specialized professional individual in my work with her. Much of my response was stilted and stereotyped. The case, from my point of view, betrays ineptness more than competence. It reflects a fumbling persistence on the part of a pastor in his efforts to help a parishioner who had a baffling, interpersonal problem.

In that respect, the case may well be typical of many counseling pastors, who are often and continually up against seemingly impossible interpersonal entanglements. But—and here is my point —in spite of every limitation on my part as a counseling pastor, the parish provided the place of the healing gesture. I was not on my own. I had resources within the community of care beyond anything that is now available to me when I counsel as a specialist.

THE PARISH SETTING

As I have suggested, the very setting of the local parish itself is invaluable. In a more extensive way than that reflected by Hiltner and Colston, I see the minister's counseling relationship embedded in a wide variety of contacts. There are the church family, worship services, small study groups, committee meetings, and social and casual contacts in the community. Somewhat in contrast to the specialist, the counseling pastor tends to relate to persons with whom he is working in counseling in other continuous and sustaining ways.

Because of the demands of a parish, the minister can seldom spend extended periods of time with any one individual. Except in unusual circumstances, if a person has not shown significant improvement within the course of six to ten individual interviews, referral to the specialist ought to be made. Such a ceiling, though, is more than compensated for by the potentially therapeutic elements of the community of faith itself. Although the face-to-face relationship is highly structured and focused directly upon the individual's needs, there is always the larger setting out of which the person comes and back into which he moves. There is more of an emphasis or overtone on the *personal* undergirding and not solely on the professional counseling.

The following excerpts underscore aspects of the setting itself as being therapeutic:

Discussion Groups

"The discussion group," the woman stated, "has certainly been something I couldn't have dispensed with. I—I just think that—ah—you just have to communicate with somebody at a deep level. If it is impossible for you to communicate with your husband—at any level, but certainly not a deep level, then, in order *to develop further,* you have to have that with somebody. The discussion group has certainly filled that need with me."

Preaching

"Your sermons," she continued, "help so much. You sit here like a mummy and you won't say a word while I'm here, but I can go to church and I can find out some of your values and some of the ways you look at things, and that, of course, would be entirely impossible with a psychiatrist."

As a specialist now and with more maturity both as a person and as a counselor, my style has modified from those days so long ago. I am more active. I do say more. I take more initiative. Yet I also wait for the other. I also allow the pressure of silence to drive forth the anxiousness lurking beneath the surface. I also insist that the other be responsible for himself. But all this is after the fact.

She pursued her point about learning of my convictions and values: "After I am in a state where I can *hear* things, I can hear from other people casual remarks and things that I read in books and I can get help that way because I apply it to myself. But I don't get dependent either because somebody has told me about me—or antagonistic because they have *criticized* me. I can take other things or leave them as I like. I can apply them to myself if I want to or I can say they don't fit me."

"In other words," I inquired, "this would apply to my preaching then? Whereas, if I said here what I say there, you could react positively or negatively—"

"That's right," she interrupted.

"—either way, becoming dependent," I reflected.

"Yes," she replied.

General Openness in Congregation

She shifted from my preaching to the atmosphere within the congregation. Although she was speaking of my impact specifically, it should be understood that my approach reflected and was reinforced by a strong group of the membership.

"I know that a lot of people don't require the amount of time that you have given me. On the other hand, a lot of people may require more time. But I do know," she emphasized, "that you have made this church, as I've told you before, so different . . . because people are more people than they used to be. For the ones who need it the most, I think that this kind of encounter is the only answer. For others, the discussion groups fill the need.

"I don't know about the others," she mused. "I don't know that they get it to the extent that their lives are completely changed."

"But apparently," I reflected, "you are saying that even *they* somehow feel more—"

"Open. That's right. More open," she continued.

"How," I wanted to know, both as a matter of genuine curiosity in creating conditions of caring and probably for my own narcissistic needs as well, "does this happen?"

"Well," she began, a bit perplexed by my obtuseness, "because you're more open. And it's so—it's so remarkable—that you aren't hurried. I don't see how in the world you ever achieve that, because I know how many things you have on your mind. Yet, we meet you somewhere and you act as if you were on vacation. And—that makes it so nice for anybody who wants to say something to you. Because if you acted as if you were in a rush to get somewhere, well, they couldn't say what they have to say to you. And even if it's not important, it's communication that—that means something to them."

Because I wanted to clear up the fact that *I tended to feel* rushed most of the time yet respond to *her experience* of my being unhurried with people, my response was rather faltering:

"So just kind of—well, you know—having time—or not even having time—at least, not trying to be several places at one time—"

"Oh that," she picked up the real point about presence and the gesture of care, "I wish I could ever achieve. I doubt if I do, but I'll struggle. About living fully in the moment, I think that's the greatest idea. But I can't do it, not by a long shot."

"But you're saying," I kept trying to make my point, "this is something that helps people feel like people."

"Certainly. You give your entire attention to them right now. And that certainly makes people more people," she concluded.

Casual Contacts

To be present to another requires being in the presence of the other. As pastor, I was continuously in the presence of others. I was potentially accessible to her as a human being.

"Another thing," she wanted to get across, "is that I'm sure you get to feel about a psychiatrist that he is your friend, but I'm certain that it's not on the level which I feel that I am your *friend,* because we see each other just in normal social situations."

She began to recall several such occasions. "Another time, I remember, when I was just so full of joy and appreciation, was one time—it must have been a Sunday School party, a Sunday School teachers' party, or something of the sort—you came to me at this meeting and said, 'How are you getting along?' and so forth. And, and that meant such a lot because you went out of your way to do this. It wasn't just in the mingling of the people. Ah, it was, oh, a private affair between us. And you really wanted to know how I was doing."

These excerpts convey something of the sustaining community setting in which the pastor works with individuals. He has a variety of avenues with which to approach and keep in touch with those with whom he is working more intimately. There are so many reinforcing gestures:

—small exploring groups in which people share deeply;

—experiences of worship and preaching in which people are held by the liturgy and informed by the sermons;

—widening and deepening openness and trust among members;

—spontaneous personal contact even in the midst of a Sunday School party.

These gestures converge to create a therapeutic milieu that supports, sustains, and strengthens the individual. He or she experiences and is part of a community seeking to exemplify care.

FREEDOM FOR PASTORAL INITIATIVE

Second only to the setting in significance is the initiative the minister can take in reaching out for contact. He is free to move toward people in ways that are permissible for no other professional person. He can enter a situation without having to justify his presence. Such mobility is gaining attention by other professional people in the mental health field. They, too, are seeking ways to leave their offices in order to get out on the streets and into the homes, where the people are.

I went to the home of the woman with whom I was working. She had not specifically invited me, except by having spoken to me briefly about family tension. I had let her know that I saw that the only help for her family was that of her seeking help for herself. Having made the contact, I had then waited. I had allowed the thought to germinate. I had waited until she herself felt ready to respond. Then I visited her at her home.

Going to Others

The following excerpts emphasize what pastoral initiative means to someone who wants help:

"I'll never forget, never, never forget," she reiterated, "the first time you came and asked me whether I had thought more about therapy. I had already told you about John's refusing to go to a psychiatrist. And you had propounded the idea, which was a kind of shock to me, that *I* should. I had never even thought of that before. And then, when you went out of your way to come just to ask me whether I'd thought any more about that, that meant more than almost anything. Because that meant that you really had concern for our family; that you had put your whole heart into it; and that you saw no solution to the problem unless I did the changing. So that a little later, when something happened which was the last straw, that made it so easy for me, so awfully much easier for me, to come to you and say, 'I have to have help.' "

Clearly, the thought that she might have contributed to the family difficulties had not occurred to her. As a caring friend and perceived by her to be a competent professional, I could raise the question of her role. I could inquire again if she had weighed the possibility.

"Because I had gone out to you—"

"Because you had gone out to me—" she reiterated. "That is the kind of thing that's, that's just priceless to anybody who's abjectly unhappy and seeing no possible way out."

Standing Apart from Others

But to go out to someone must never be confused with grabbing hold of that person. The gesture of pastoral initiative requires both movement *and* detachment. Even as the counseling pastor can take initiative with his parishioners, so also he respects their ability to assume responsibility. He does not move in and tell them what they should do. He avoids detailing how they ought to act. Instead, he confronts them with his perceptions. He speculates on possible alternatives. He pinpoints pain that needs facing.

The following exchange describes something of this paradox of helping yet not helping:

"I think that it is just wonderful that you *don't* help more." She stressed the word 'don't.' "How in the world you can keep from it at times is more than I *know* because—"

"What do you mean," I wondered, "that I *don't* help more?"

"Well, that you don't say things that would illumine the situation a little bit because—even since—even since I have had this—ah —completely revolutionary experience, which gives me new eyes and new ears, I can see other people in the light—a *little* bit in the light in which you have seen me, and I see that I mustn't say what I see because you didn't, because," she laughed, "help would hurt sometimes." I joined her in laughing. "So I think you are simply wonderful because you don't *say* anything."

Frankly, I did not say anything most of the time simply because I did *not know* what to say. If I had had a thought in my head, I would have expressed it. Even so, the way she stated the matter of help intrigued me.

"But wouldn't it help if I did say something?"

"Well, you would think it would help at the moment, you really—I mean, I would have thought at the moment that it would help if you would just give me a little nudge or something when I was stuck. But in the long run it would not help."

"Why not?" By now I was most curious. We had never touched on this topic before.

"Because I have to be—I have to make my own decisions.
I have to learn that I am—adult and—and that there isn't
anybody else who's *ever* going to make my decisions for me."

I could have said something if I had had anything to say *and*
still have allowed her to make her own decisions. Perhaps if I
had known more, I could have taken some of the edge off
the pain of being stuck. Yet her point stands. In the final act
she had to stand apart from everyone.

While the pastoral counselor must leave initiative to the one
seeking help, the counseling pastor can take initiative himself.
He can go to the person and stand by him. In short, he is mobile,
even while he is respecting the person's right to self-determination.
This does not mean that he must remain as verbally passive as
the woman felt I had remained. More might have been done to
get at the characterological nature of her behavior, but that is
secondary to the importance of the combination of mobility and
detachment of the counseling pastor. The pastor can move in and
out of persons' lives with a freedom that increases the possibilities
available to no other helping professional.

PARISH REALITIES

In stressing the strength of the parish context, I am not un-
mindful of its realities. Its realities, however, may not be quite
as many perceive them. It is to these unanticipated realities that
I wish now to direct your attention.

One characteristic of counseling in the parish presents a dis-
cordant note. We cannot count on success. Not only is it possible
that a parishioner's difficulties may not clear up but, even more
likely, they may not dramatically deteriorate. They may simply
hang on as chronic disturbance.

The picture of chronic heartache is obviously not restricted to
the parish and to the counseling pastor. What is likely to be confined to the parish and to the counseling pastor, however, is the
perplexity of such unmitigated pain. We often live with tragic,
seemingly unsolvable, situations.

The woman in my parish found better ways of coping with her
life, notwithstanding her conflicts festered for years without resolution. At times her discouragement almost overwhelmed her.
When she could look back over a year's period, she would recognize that there had been a *little* movement. In the midst of such

broken relationships the minister experiences the necessity and the demand to stand beside those who are hurting even when he sees no way out. His decision to stay with the brokenness is for him a major principle.

Unlike other helping professionals, the counseling pastor has an ongoing relationship beyond that of temporary help. He is continually confronted by the tragic consequences of others' failure to act decisively. The excerpts that follow demonstrate the unrelieved burden of chronic pain. The feeling is a common one.

"There is no question about the fact that John has—progressed. I don't know how to say how much because it's over—such a long period of time, that unless I look back even a *whole* year," she accentuated the word whole, "I can't see any improvement. So—I just can only say that there has been improvement. He is no longer—*completely* tied up in knots *all* the time. And he has taken responsibilities," her voice dropped as from loss of conviction, "some responsibilities. And he has found—some enjoyments and—"

She was almost trying to talk herself into believing that life had changed.

"—so—I don't think that it's hopeless, but good gracious, I don't know how long it takes—"

The weariness weighed heavily upon her.

"A year seems such a terrible long time. And when, for instance, last September came—after the September before when I had said this is the end, this is—this has to be entirely different and I'm not putting up with anything anymore; this is the end. Well, he wouldn't accept the fact that it was the end and he refused a divorce, saying that it was for the sake of making a home for our three children, which was not the real reason; but anyway, that's what he said—well then, a year from that time, I thought that *surely* there would be big progress. Well, of course, just about a year ago now is when I reached the lowest ebb of all, as you," she was experiencing frenzied discouragement as she cleared her throat, "can surely remember, that I was just going to get another apartment and I had had enough and there was just no other way to do it. I was simply going to walk out and—so I am glad—I guess—that I didn't do that."

I experienced her as running out of conviction. "You aren't quite sure, though?" I asked.

"Well," she acknowledged, "I think it depends upon how this thing finally comes out. Because the longer it drags on, the harder it is to do that. Last June I was really ready to do it, emotionally and every other way." As she cleared her throat, I sensed unrelenting heartache. "Now the longer that it drags on, the harder it is going to be—to do that thing which I could have done last June."

Aloud, I wondered why she had not left as she claimed she had been ready to do.

"I didn't because—you helped me not."

That took me by surprise. Had I stopped her?

"No, you didn't stop me. But I felt surely that you thought it was not a hopeless situation. And if it was not a hopeless situation, I did not want to do anything drastic."

She lapsed back into quietness. After a few minutes she plodded on, "I understand that we revert to the past and that things are not always going to go onward and upward, but there are such tiny little—successes, and then, such *great* reversions to the past, that it's *mighty* discouraging."

By now the feeling of discouragement flooded her earlier stance of improvement.

"Which raises the question," I tried gently to point out, "in your mind whether you should keep on or not." Actually, I had *not* held the conviction it was not a hopeless situation.

"Yes—whether we're really going to arrive anywhere in the end," she said. Discouragement pervaded everything.

The fact that I myself had felt uncertain as to which way to "nudge" her—whether to stay or to go—had allowed the pain to continue as chronic. Yet, I am convinced that no one from the outside can know for another what the other wants and does not want. What I might find intolerable to live with, another might choose as the lesser of two pains. Thus, the counseling pastor stays with the one seeking help in terms of that person's ultimate longings, hoping that out of the supporting relationship some clarity of direction might come. Here the woman saw the supporting relationship as being on the side of maintaining the marriage. That was not my conscious intent. However, my silence allowed her own longings for hope and her own ambivalence to be read into me and my attitude. She found in me what was latent in herself.

A more sophisticated counseling approach conceivably might have produced resolution. I might have engaged in family therapy, seeing the family as a family rather than the wife in isolation. That would have encouraged each member to reflect upon and articulate what he saw and felt about the family's hurting. I might have asked the reluctant husband to come in *to help me* understand his wife's difficulties. But I had concluded on the basis of what she had reported to me about her husband and the oldest child and from my own observations that either approach likely would be rejected. Concerning the marriage and family difficulties, only an unsatisfactory neurotic pattern persisted.

Most people, including professionals, want life to be neat and tidy. The counseling specialist can close a case and put it back into his files. He may conclude that the person was not ready for help or that he exhibited too much resistance. Regardless of the reaction of his patient, he hastens to write "finished" over the situation.

As a counseling pastor, though, I saw my woman patient every Sunday in church. I met her on the street. I sat with her in meetings. I could not ignore her heartache. I could not forget her discouragement. I had to stay with the ambiguity. I had to live with the ambivalence. That is part of the reality of what the *real* gesture is all about.

GROWTH IN SPITE OF . . .

The physical environment, however, is never quite the same as the experienced world. Even in the midst of the deadening, growth can take place. Externals remain the same; inner reality undergoes transformation.

In spite of everything the woman was experiencing, she found within herself a deepened sense of who she was and a heightened sense of meaning in life. In that respect, the counseling pastor probably participates in the realization of larger goals than the counselor who has a more restricted relationship.

Of necessity the specialist focuses upon relieving neurotic tension and anxiety, assimilating dissociated experience, and reestablishing clearer contact with the environment. Many specialists hold to goals that go beyond these. They seek so to free the individual from the anxiety arising from disturbances in his interpersonal relationships that he may creatively experience and courageously handle the anxiety fundamental to being human. By participating in that basic anxiety, the individual begins to experience his own authenticity. In that process the personal relationship between the one seeking help and the one giving help goes beyond the strictly professional experience, even though that special structure is basic in the encounter.

These wider areas of inner growth and outer concern are especially available within the parish context. Even in a chronic disturbance the gesture of the place of care makes a difference.

"When I heard Bach's *Mass in B Minor,*" she reported, picking up the imagery of the setting, "the first three parts of that were extremely meaningful to me, because it was the story of my therapy. The *Kyrie*, the cry for help from the bottom of my soul, and then the *Gloria,* when I had finally done something and proclaimed the fact that *I* was *I* and was never going to be anyone else, and the devil take the hindmost, really, and then after that period of exaltation, there was a *Credo* when I could affirm what was real and true and determine truth from ego." She had telescoped the process. "That was a wonderful, exulting experience to me. I don't even know what the Catholic mass is supposed to be, but, if that's it, it can have great meaning."

"It sort of summed up your whole experience," I said.

"It did."

"You know," I wanted to clear up my own puzzlement about the process, "one of the things—that I'm a bit confused about is— your feeling this frustration and—misery and discouragement and so on. Yet all the time you talk about this—revolutionary experience—I'm not sure how these are related or what this revolutionary experience is or how it's really changed anything since—you know—in some ways the pattern seems to be the same."

"That's discouraging, isn't it?" she asked.

"No," I hastened to defend my uncertainty about the growth she reported. "I'm just—I'm—I'm not saying it's discouraging." Actually, I was saying it was discouraging as well as puzzling. Such denials are usually affirmations. "I'm trying to understand what—what the revolutionary experience means to you in— relationship to your home situation."

"Well, I think it means that *I'm growing,* Jim, and I haven't arrived anywhere." Her strength came through with power.

"But it certainly means that I have more perspective than I used to have, and it certainly means that I'm a lot more open than I used to be. In fact, the whole world looks different to me now than it used to."

"In what kinds of ways?" I wanted to know. Were there solid evidences or was she just talking?

"Well—I've always known that everybody had their troubles—but now I'm an awful lot more perceptive about other people's troubles and more able to do something about them. In fact, one of the most glorious feelings, and glorious isn't the word because I feel terribly humble, but I guess I feel glorious at the same time, is the fact that a few times I've been able to do something for somebody else that mattered to them, because they told me afterwards that it did matter. And I wasn't trying to do something big and wonderful for them. But I was *able* to and that was just—simply out of this world!—that I—I, who am so bottled up, could—could do anything—"

There *were* evidences to support her affirmation of transformation!

"And I wasn't—I wasn't trying to do something big and wonderful for them. You know?" Her awesome joy kept spilling over. "But I was *able* to. And that was just—simply out of this world—that I can go out to people and perceive their need. I guess the thing that you are asking me about is that—I am still me. Well—"

"Yes. And yet, you have said and really communicated to me that—that some kind of change took place," I commented.

"Well, a terrific change. My—my whole world got bright! The colors are different! It was just as—if I had been seeing through a mirror darkly."

She was experiencing the world more sharply, more clearly, more fully. Even though she knew pain, she knew exultation. Even though she felt discouraged, she experienced dignity. That quality of dignity seemed to be part of the power of the transformation.

"It happened," she explained in response to my question of how the change came about, "because I found that I had worth—I didn't have to try to be what I thought people ought to be—That is, just put up with things that I thought you couldn't do anything about. Pretend that it was all right, though I knew absolutely that it wasn't all right, and, therefore, I came to the place where I could not even pretend it was all right anymore."

"So somehow," I was groping to catch hold of the crucial clue,"—a—feeling that you didn't have to pretend anymore, even though the external situation didn't change, at least being honest about what the situation was—was the revolutionary experience. Is that it?"

"Well, yes. I suppose, just to put it in a nutshell, I found out that I—am a person of worth—who—can express myself, even though what I say or do is not going to be acceptable to other people. And—that took a lot of courage for me to come to that."

She paused to take a breath. "Now I've found out that even if I continue in a situation that is far from ideal, that it is not throttling me, because I am me and I am not going to be throttled!" She finished with firmness!

Growth clearly took root in the experience of autonomy and dignity. As she experienced *her* responsiveness, she found she did not have to be a passive victim of an indifferent or hostile environment. Instead, she could take initiative; she could set limits; she could be as she wanted to be. While the outer environment continued as before, her *experienced* world took on more personal significance.

Even more crucial, though, was the way growth spread beyond the confines of her private inner world to the larger world of others. She grew more sensitive to where others were; she found ways to be with them in ways that mattered to them. From my having been "present" for her, she became "present" for others. She found her confirmation in ministering to others.

Other than the counseling pastor, no helping professional has such access to the inner world of people. No other helping professional is so accessible to others.

The local parish provides the context for *real* gestures of "being for others." Nothing need be extraneous; everything can be integral. The counseling pastor can move into contact without specific invitation. By sensitive presence he can assist individuals to acknowledge crisis and respond. The gesture of a group—the gesture of a meeting—the gesture of a pastoral prayer—the gesture of a fleeting touch—the gesture of an open people—such gestures make for healing!

Even though the pastor cannot avoid living with unfinished situations, his people can, and do, grow in their inner lives. They gain in their capacity to shape their worlds and not merely be shaped by them.

The counseling pastor invariably sees himself in relation to the historic reality of the Christian church. He is, first of all, a minister of the gospel of reconciliation and secondarily a counselor or troubled people. He cannot divorce himself from his concrete embeddedness in the local parish. Therefore, he works with individuals, and those individuals are always in transition. They can never be lifted completely out of the community of care. Rather, he aids them to find their own ways back into truer community.

Ultimate purpose and penultimate means converge. Vital communication is reestablished, at least with some. Communion with a human community of faith transcends many barriers. The local parish discloses the place of genuine gestures of care.

demonstrating-being-in-this-world

What has brought us together?
Trouble. . . . We both are in
trouble. We belong . . . or we
wouldn't be here.

. . . ah, the energy we spend
hiding from one another, afraid
as we are of being identified.
But here we are, identified. . . .

A great piece of luck
provided we know how to use it:

no longer any need to worry about the picture
we present—free to find out who we
truly are.

If we know that no one can dislodge us.
Truman Capote [1]

Five

Thee and Me

Ordeal with chaos. . . .
Losing one's mind and coming to one's senses. . . .
Agony and ecstasy in the parish context. . . .

How delicately intertwined are the personal and the public, the intimate and the institutional, what happens within and what transpires without!

GROWTH IN RELATIONSHIP

Look again, if you will, at Giacometti's sculpture of *Three Men Walking*. These figures poignantly project our contemporary experience of loneliness. Look more closely at the feet of each of the figures; follow the lines of their movement. What do you discover?

They are walking past each other; their paths will never meet; they have lost human contact!

Here is a dramatic portrayal of the way in which we seem to come together and yet, in fact, never touch. Our paths approach each other, yet never intersect. What ironic tragedy—physical closeness without personal presence.

Proximity, however, makes presence potentially possible. *Metanoia* (change, turning, reorientation, refocusing): if those figures turned toward one another, they could meet! Relationship with other human beings is basic to an individual's becoming human. What goes on between a thee and a me provides the soil in which the roots of our lives take hold and receive nourishment. We cannot grow in isolation. Who I am meets who you are or we are both lost!

The Loss of Life

Studies of children who have been lost from the human community and reared among animals demonstrate what happens when the paths of our lives do not intersect.[1] When those youngsters were found, captured, and domesticated, they proved unable to adapt. When put on a civilized diet, they developed dysentery and, in many cases, died. When spoken to, they could only grunt with the gutteral limitations of the animals that raised them.

Research on the effects of deprivation in young children leaves no doubt as to the necessity for basic trust and free access between persons.[2] The effects of being deprived of mothering care include:

> poorer school achievement
> less ability to develop relationships
> a greater incidence of problem behavior
> marked restlessness
> incapacitating fears
> abnormal cravings for affection.

Unanticipated findings in experimental work with monkeys in the Primate Laboratory at the University of Wisconsin further corroborate the consequences of the loss of contact.

Those young monkeys were raised by wood-and-wire substitute mothers. At first these cloth covered images seemed preferable to natural mothers. They were constantly available. They never scolded or cuffed or rejected the infant as real mothers sometimes did. Normally, monkeys exhibit complex behavior patterns and strong group ties. These monkeys, however, disclosed striking deficiencies in both their behavior patterns and their group relations.

> Their play remains at an infantile level. Encounters between them have an almost accidental quality, as though one monkey didn't know what to do when it met another. Attempts to breed the surrogate-raised monkeys have also been wholly unsuccessful; the monkeys—male and female —simply don't know how they are supposed to behave when mating season starts.[3]

At the beginning of life the lack of intersecting paths is disastrous for monkeys as well as humans. In later years, loneliness and isolation continue to reap havoc. "It is a rare person," observed Harry Stack Sullivan, who can do without human contact "for long spaces of time without undergoing a deterioration of personality." [4] People become patients and inmates because they lack the most critical factor for fulfilling their needs, namely, a person whom they genuinely care about and who they feel genuinely cares for them.[5] As Genesis reminds us, man was not made to be alone. "It is not good that man should be alone" (Genesis 2:18).

We cannot be human without other humans. We cannot be people without other people. We cannot grow without each other growing.

The Gift of Life

The deep necessity of relationship depends more upon what we *are* to each other than upon what we say to each other. Something of the pathos of our paths not crossing and the relief of discovering that our paths can intersect is revealed in a schizophrenic girl's description of her experience with her therapist:

> Meeting you made me feel like a traveler who's been lost in a land where no one speaks his language. Worst of all, the traveler doesn't even know where he should be going. He feels completely lost and helpless and alone. Then, suddenly, he meets a stranger who can speak English. Even if the stranger doesn't know the way to go, it feels so much better to be able to share the problem with someone, to have him understand how badly you feel. If you're not alone, you don't feel helpless anymore. Somehow it gives you life and a willingness to fight again.[6]

The surest way to transform lostness and loneliness and alienation into belongingness, relationship, and fulfillment is through intersecting paths. As we disclose who we are, we become who we are. As we give, we grow. The capacity to be depends upon our capacity to cross paths with others.

Evidence has converged from research in counseling and psychotherapy. Embedded within the multitude of approaches with their comparable effectiveness lies the source of personal change, specifically the personal relationship between the helper and the helped.[7] The central ingredients in that relationship are:

ACCURATE EMPATHY: sensitivity to what the other is experiencing and communicating that understanding in a way that resonates with the other.[8]

NONPOSSESSIVE WARMTH: "accepting [the other] as a person with human potentialities . . . valuing [him] as a person, separate from any evaluation of his behavior or thoughts." [9]

GENUINENESS: "direct personal encounter, meeting on a person-to-person basis, without defensiveness or a retreat into facades or roles. . . ." [10]

These qualities, which evidence suggests are teachable, make for effectiveness in our relationships with one another regardless of the goals involved.[11]

As a coteacher of a third-grade church school class, growth in the children demanded that I participate with them in what we were about. That required that my personal path had to cross their personal paths in some self-giving, self-disclosing, appropriate way. Knowledge for life comes from knowledge of life and not only knowledge about life. I had to be involved personally with them —somehow—if what we were about were to convey life.

The first session of a new class in the fall provided a means of sensing who each of us was and how our paths might intersect. To do that, all of us made individual posters—collages—designed to portray who we were through what was important to us. The children pasted cats and dogs, cars and gerbils, books and bats. To allow my path to intersect their paths, I had to enter into a genuine, two-way process myself. Frankly, I felt silly cutting and pasting; but I also felt *the demand to be real.*

I threw myself into the project with gusto. My wife did not exactly appreciate the outcome. She is a gardener, and on the preceding day, in addition to our gardening, we had shampooed the living-room rug. Providentially, I found one advertisement that combined gardening tools and rug shampoos. My wife would have preferred a more romantic expression of our relationship, and so would I. But what I did disclosed a part of her life that would catch the attention of the children and the fact that she is important to me.

The courage to allow the human side of ourselves to show through our role responsibilities awakens the maturing process, whether it takes place in church, school, or home. Failure to let the human side of ourselves come through our role responsibilities cripples that process.

But the courage to risk ourselves in a relationship for the sake of growth uncovers a deeper issue.

So far, my discussion of thee and me has dwelt on closeness, togetherness, intimacy, and openness. A deeper look suggests a variety of interactions instead of a single interaction. Among many, there are also distance and separateness, "over againstness" and confrontation, movement toward and movement away from. Each of these interactions constitutes some form of relatedness. Relationship is neither a single nor a static quality. It is flowing process.

Growth through relationship, therefore, emerges as more subtle and complex than at its first appearance. For our purposes we shall examine the various forms of relationship in terms of three kinds of movement: toward others, against others, and away from others.[12]

MOVEMENT TOWARD OTHERS

Without my path crossing your path in some way, we can have no relationship. I must intend to be in contact with you. I must respond to you in ways that recognize your existence. I must want to meet you *as* you. Such basic intention and initiative cannot be taken for granted. Unless we openly recognize each other, our paths will never intersect.

After a church service an informal conversation between an eighth-grade girl and the junior high worker lays out obstacles to contacting and opportunities for meeting.

As the worker walked through the sanctuary, he came upon Nancy sitting alone in a back pew. He spoke first.

"Hi, again. I thought you'd gone home."

"I was waiting for you." She seemed nervous and unsure; yet she made clear that she wanted their paths to cross.

"You want to see me?" He was making certain he got her message. She really was making a move toward him.

"Yes, there's something I have to talk over with someone." She might have talked to others; she had chosen to talk with him. Over the previous two years in the junior high fellowship they had developed a warm relationship. Now she wanted specific help. "I'm afraid to talk to the minister," she whispered, mouth trembling and eyes averted, "but I know I'll have to."

Her request was intended to evoke his help and support. He responded, "Okay. Let's find a quiet place." With that he led her to an isolated room in the church. She said nothing.

Once there, she spoke more confidently. "I guess you're the only one I know to talk to. I don't know how to say what I have to say to the minister. I hope you can help me. I can talk to you, but I don't think I could talk to any minister right now."

"I guess ministers seem to scare you," he reflected.

"Yes, they do—I don't know how to say this to the minister, but—I don't want to join the church this year." She sat very quietly, caught up in her fearfulness of the confession.

The youth worker realized she wanted to make contact, not only with him but even more with the minister. She was acting *in order for* her path to intersect his path. So the worker merely nodded his head, acknowledging her announcement without evaluation, "Mmm-hmm."

After a long pause she began to unravel the issue. "It's just that—well—I don't really know how to say it. Joining the church isn't as simple as I've always thought it would be. I mean—you really have to want to work to be a part of it." The emotional magnitude again set her mouth trembling. "It—it isn't something you take lightly. You commit all you have to it."

She saw the seriousness of a deliberate decision to make a commitment. He recognized her uncertainty, and said, "And you don't feel you're ready to make this kind of commitment?"

They talked of her discovering the seriousness of the step. She told of not knowing how to tell the minister. Her trouble with authority figures came out as she described being afraid of him in the membership class and of feeling stranded by her parents in their lack of support for her in the process.

"They signed the letter saying they would go through the Membership Class lessons with me, but they haven't helped me at all. They just leave me alone to do it by myself. Even when I ask them questions, they won't help me," she related.

"Sounds like you're having trouble in making them notice that you're around," he commented.

With that understanding response, Nancy moved more deeply into what was eating at her. She resented not being treated as an individual and chafed at the attention her sisters received. The youth worker sought to do more than merely comfort. He tried to focus on the reality.

"Have you ever talked to your parents about how you feel?" he asked.

"No, I haven't." Nancy winced at the reality; her mouth again started trembling. "But I don't think I can talk to them. They always seem to be too busy to talk with me. I can't get their attention." With that she could hold back the tears no longer. They poured down her cheeks. The youth worker waited, quietly and acceptingly. She pulled herself together and went on, "I just can't talk with them. I mean, we can't even discuss anything. I talk with my mother and she cuts me off short. And I try to argue something with her and she gives me her opinion and that's that. All she ever says when she can't answer me is, 'It's so because I said it's so.' And whenever I want to do something and she doesn't want me to do it, she'll say, 'No,' and I'll ask 'Why?' Then she'll say, 'Because I'm your mother, that's why!' "

"My dad doesn't say anything to me." Nancy then moved the topic of distance to the other authority in her life. "He just goes off and reads the paper. I don't see him much at all. He's away at work before I leave for school, and he's usually busy doing something during the evenings. Even when he is home, he doesn't talk to me or want to help me. I mean, well, this is why I can't really get my homework done for the Membership Class."

Again her mouth quivered from emotion. After a few more minutes of conversation she pulled herself together. "Thank you," she smiled, "I feel much better now. I think I can talk to the minister about this. I'd like to see him before I leave. Would you walk to his office with me?" She had moved from dependency to initiative.[13]

With that they set off to make her next contact!

The minister had been walking past Nancy; Nancy had been walking past the minister. The parents had been walking past Nancy; Nancy had been walking past her parents. Paths did not intersect. Only as Nancy felt the need to alter her direction *and* acted did their paths begin to intersect.

But such intended movement toward relationship ought not to be made lightly. We need to ask quite realistically:

DO I REALLY WANT TO MOVE INTO CONTACT WITH OTHERS?

Am I prepared to put myself at the disposal of others as

Christ put himself at the disposal of others?

Am I really prepared to show intelligent outgoing concern for others' well-being, apart from my own well-being?

Am I really prepared to risk my own certainties, my own securities, my own becoming as the relationship develops?

Am I really prepared to be guided by the givenness of the other instead of playing with my own fantasied possibilities of how I would like that person to be?

Again I illustrate from my third-grade church school class. One Sunday our lesson lifted up the apostle Paul's predicament: what I want to do, I don't do; what I don't want to do, that I do. We explored our various kinds of mixed feelings—ugly feelings, angry feelings, mad feelings, bad feelings. Then we tried to show how these feelings *felt* by finger painting. And by "we" I mean "we"—all of us, each of us, messing in the gooey paint, sliding our hands over the wet paper, creating monsters and meanings, only to wipe them out as other expressions flowed through our hands.

Some chose black, others, brown; I chose red. One very quiet, nice, well-behaved boy chose orange—bright, yet not too bright, soft, yet not washed-out. His whole paper radiated a lovely orange without any discernible finger streaks. Then, unobtrusively, in the center of that bland pleasantness he fingered a Nazi swastika! For an instant he let us see his buried yet real feelings of anger. With our having seen and his having said, he quickly wiped it out. Only the undisturbed orange surface remained. Yet our paths had crossed. We both knew the hurt and the hate lurking below the nice and the quiet.

Because we had moved toward that boy, he began to move toward us. He let us see a fierce and frightening part of himself. Through our relationship in class he started to grow; he loosened an old pattern of quiet control. By so doing, a new pattern of more open rebellion could slip out. Because we could see him more clearly, he could experience himself more fully. As he could experience himself more fully, we were forced to modify our preconceived ideas. In wanting to be in contact with the deeper side of his being, we were required to risk our own settledness for the sake of truer wholeness.

The next Sunday he again finger painted with orange. This time, though, he kept streaking the Nazi swastika in and streaking it out. Finally, he stroked it in, drew a circle around it and left it that way. He had taken the risk of saying, in effect, "Anger is part of me and I don't have to hide it." When we had a parents' program, that boldly circled swastika hung on the wall along with the other posters.

In moving toward others, there come sudden, spontaneous, intuitive encounters. Sometimes there comes the recognition of unsuspected and disturbing depths of anger, as with that boy. Sometimes there comes doubt about desirable goals, as with that junior high girl. At other times there comes "an immediate sense of relatedness, an immediate feeling of harmony and communion." [14]

I remember a seminary student who carefully kept a distance between us. In class there would be the calculating gaze; in the hall there would be the formal nod. One day when I walked into class, everything had changed. Not a word was spoken, but a glance was exchanged. Our eyes met; we spoke without speaking; there was a sudden dropping of convention; there came a letting go, a giving in, an open responsive give-and-take. Now we could be serious; now we could be playful; now we could be grave; now we could struggle. No longer did our paths miss; now they intersected.

In another class I had been pressing the students as to where they were in their lives. One was anchored right to the chair in that room. Another was back in her apartment fretting over the mess in her kitchen.

Then, suddenly and unexpectedly, one said, "I'm in Granville, where you were minister. I'm remembering the funeral service you had for my mother. I don't remember anything you said, but I remember you and what you meant to me."

In that moment the class grew quiet; restlessness vanished; a reverential awe engulfed us. Our paths had intersected. We had connected. And because of that relationship each of us in the class became a bit more than we had been.

For growth we need to move toward each other in a relationship that recognizes and encounters each other's humanness. Thee and me! Yet because of the risk of disrupting our settledness by the presence of doubts about desirable decisions, angry swastikas, or intimate caring, we need to ask:

> Do I really want to move toward others?
> Do I really want our paths to intersect?

As I have intimated, it is not enough simply to move toward each other. The intimacy, the closeness, the meeting of thee and me can easily dissolve into what one student termed "sloppy agape." For fullness of life our paths likewise need to move against each other and apart from each other.

MOVEMENT AGAINST OTHERS

Events of the last decade have torn open and ripped up the middle-class bias and the middle-class conditioning that equate challenging directness and honesty in communication with an aggressive, hostile, and destructive attack.[15] When Timothy Leary and his associates sought to find words to express adaptive aggression or maladaptive affiliation, they could uncover few such words. The English language appears insensitive to the concept of "socially approved hostility" except for such words as "frank," "blunt," or "critical." Nor could they find terms for "extreme, rigid, maladjustive affectionate behavior."[16] Yet we now realize there is both a place for and the necessity of movement against others.

Once we move into a caring relationship with another, neither of us can be allowed to evade recognizing what he is doing or his responsibility for it. Confrontation is the language of interpersonal relationships for such a move. Judgment is the language of theology for the move. Regardless of expression the experience is the same. There is an unhealthy gap between what a person experiences and what he communicates. There is a conflict between knowing and doing, between the expectation and the reality. There is dissonance between the music one plays and the music one can play. While the person is accepted, such discrepancy is not.

In moving against others we interrupt manipulative and maladaptive behavior. The confrontation calls into question the unlimited extension and endless expression of another. It constitutes what in cybernetics is called negative feedback, that is, information warning one that he is off-course and needs to correct for faulty direction. It is the ultimate means of precipitating a crisis or facilitating a choice point by bringing the other in touch with himself and confronting him with alternatives and their implications.[17]

The Greek word for judgment is *krisis*. It reflects the reorienting possibilities within life that is off-balance. *Krisis* does not convey the unfortunate connotation of disaster; instead it focuses upon critical possibilities. At its best it points toward an impersonally valid objective reality, even as Amos suggests with his image, "Behold, I am setting a plumb line in the midst of my people Israel" (Amos 7:8).

An interchange between a student and myself illustrates the movement against others *in order for* life to be awakened. We were in a series of small-group meetings. Initially there had been only five of us. After the first meeting four others joined the group. In the fourth meeting, after a brief break in the two-hour stretch, several students questioned the value of the preceding hour.

A student who had had a quarter of clinical pastoral education spoke: "I don't know. I didn't like the conversation because no one was honest. I mean no one would really say what he thought. I really don't want to bring it in, but we had a great experience in clinical training this summer, and I want to share it with everyone and have everyone feel it, too. But I have tried not to bring in my training. I really don't want to—"

He had been talking *at* others in this passive-aggressive manner ever since the four new members had appeared. His insistence that he did not want to "lord it over" others because of his training was actually a way of bringing it in without assuming responsibility for it.

Such a response tends to provoke aggression and rejection in return. Instead I shifted the interaction to more direct confrontation. "Yes, you do want to bring in your training."

"No, I don't." He defended his intentions while resisting my interpretation. "I remember what I got out of the training, but I don't want to bring it in."

"Yes, you do—" I pressed my interpretation.

"No, I don't. Well, maybe I do, but don't realize it." He began to acknowledge a discrepancy between what he was saying and what he was communicating. "But I wish everyone would be honest and really say what he thinks."

"Why don't you start?" I demanded. "What do you want to say?" He had been saying that he wanted others to be honest, but he had not said specifically, directly, and responsibly what he really wanted to get across.

"It's not me, but the others. I don't have anything to say," he objected.

"Yes, it is you." I continued to move against him. "Ever since we started, except for the first session, you have grilled and accused others. It has always been a third person singular with you. Never once have you spoken what you feel. But *you* accuse others for not doing the same thing."

I had pressed him hard, perhaps too hard, for I myself had failed to let him know of my frustration with his passive aggression.

"I really don't think that is fair, Mr. Ashbrook."

"But it is, Jack. Think how you have put everyone in this room on the carpet, but not yourself."

"Well, if I did, I didn't realize it," he said. He was right. He had been cut off from his experiencing. With the move against him he could again recover his senses. "Okay, then," he declared, "I will!" He now spoke directly to the four intruders. "The truth is that I resented you guys coming into this group. We had such a great group, just the four of us." Significantly, he had not counted me as part of the group. "There was more communication and honesty in that first session than I have ever seen at school. And then you guys came in and completely spoiled everything. I hated you for coming and wrecking it."

Now he had moved from passive bitterness to more adaptive frankness.

"That is why (he turned and looked directly at one newcomer) I guess, Ken, that I asked you the first day why you were here. It was because I wanted you out and, therefore, since I hadn't seen you in our class, I thought I might be able to get you out that way. Did you realize it?"

Because of the move against him, Jack was then able to move toward others. He could give as well as ask. He looked for feedback as to what he was really getting across. He was beginning to get back in touch with his own experience by levelling with others.

Confrontation, clearly, represents "a meeting between persons who are involved in a conflict or controversy and who remain together, face-to-face, until their feelings of divisiveness and alienation are resolved." [18] Each must maintain his own identity in the "over againstness." Part of the confusion with the surge of black-power advocates, to shift the focus to a different area, lies in the overly guilty reaction of whites. They lie down and let blacks stomp all over them. That is the worst form of disrespect—disrespect for oneself and disrespect for the other. Respect demands a refusal to buy what another sells *if* in the process one's identity is destroyed and the other's is extended beyond its proper limits.

My ability to fulfill my needs must not deprive others of their ability to fulfill their needs,[19] even as their ability to fulfill their needs must not deprive me of my ability to fulfill my needs.

In such movement against others, which must of necessity involve their movement against us as well, there comes the demand to allow difference, contrast, controversy, and hurt to erupt. There is no birth without the pangs of birth. So, the demon-possessed man cried out to Jesus, "For God's sake, don't torture me!" (Mark 5:7). Here is a misery added onto already existing misery. Such pain appears crucial to the healing relationship; yet by its presence it confuses and confounds the person crying out for help.

The movement against another need not be as aggressive as mine was against Jack. It may be disruptive by simply letting another person face the confusion lurking just below the surface.

Looking back on a pastoral counseling relationship with me, one person reflected, "Those conferences were really agony to go through, so many times. They were causing confusion and the whole thing was just completely upsetting. It wasn't just a case of coming and then leaving and then forgetting everything, because it was something that I continued to think about. And it was really quite confusing for a while and I really got so upset so many times. I'd say, 'I'm *never* going to see him anymore—I won't do it!'

"I was so confused," she emphasized, "and *so* mixed up. I *never* in my life have been more confused than the first time I came to you. I completely understood in my own mind what I wanted before I came to see you. And yet I just talked myself silly; so I didn't know—I just didn't know what I was doing or what I wanted."

Another person put the painful perplexity of "over againstness" this way: "You are *there*—utterly sincere. I'm not. You are with me, and most of the time I am not with you. You shamed me, and I'm frightened of you. I might lose control. You make me feel how insincere I really am. I want to run away from you and yet I don't."

Here we begin to sense what it is in the "over againstness" that produces the pain. It is the confrontation, the judgment: "What is the truth of your situation?" By someone's being "with" a person, the person is forced to be "with" himself.

Because of the pain, the intended movement against another cannot be taken lightly. We need to ask quite realistically:

> Am I strong enough to move against others?
>
> Am I able to face hard facts?
>
> Am I able to risk anger?
>
> Am I able to allow separateness?

In other words,

> Am I able to stand firm in the face of others' failures?
>
> Am I able to be clear in the presence of others' frenzy?
>
> Am I able to sort out the real from the unreal?
>
> Am I able to forget winning or losing and, instead, try to understand the frustrating realities and the unknown possibilities?
>
> Am I strong enough to have people furious with me for what I am or am not doing?
>
> Am I able to let others have a way of life radically different from mine yet still confront them with our differences?
>
> Can I respect the "otherness" of others even as I affirm the integrity of myself?
>
> Do I have enough identity of my own that I am not downcast by others' depression, nor sucked in by their dependency, nor frightened by their fears, nor destroyed by their bitterness?

For growth we need to move against each other in a relationship that contrasts and confronts the humanness of one another. Yet because of the risk of painful clash we need to ask:

AM I REALLY TOUGH ENOUGH to move against others?

But whatever the risk may be, the reality is there. As one parishioner wrote of our counseling/celebrating relationship:

> Maybe all the things I'd like to say can be focused on the words you use following the Scripture reading in Sunday morning worship. That dynamic challenge for response! "If you respond to these words, then *for you* they have become the Word of the Living God." No one else I've ever heard has done that, and I hope you'll never change it.
>
> I believe that is what you did to me—first acceptance, then challenge —the challenge to be myself, to be real, to be aware—or maybe just to be!

MOVEMENT APART FROM OTHERS

Growth through relationship requires not only the intimate immediacy of encounter and not only the jarring contrast of confrontation; it also demands movement apart from others.

If, like Giacometti's men walking, we need to turn in such ways that our paths intersect, we need to turn a second time so that our paths separate. To insure life, we must allow distance. Closeness is necessary for growth yet never sufficient for growth.

Against the inertia that would have kept Abraham in Ur of the Chaldeans and against the endless continuity of inherited power, God calls us to leave behind that which we have known, not only that which is undesirable but, even more, that which is worthwhile. Moses could see the Promised Land; yet he had to let others cross over to the other side. Jesus knew the Father; yet he had to depart from men for them to receive the Strengthener.[20]

The temptation for those who are helped and for those who help is to hang on to each other. Once restored to his rightful mind, the Gerasene demoniac wanted to remain with Jesus, go with him wherever he went, and be with him wherever he was. Instead, Jesus sent him back into his own situation to live the new life he had found.

That person who was so confused in our conferences initially later came to acknowledge and express the desideratum of moving apart: ". . . maybe I could use the analogy of your being like a wooden crutch. But I can't say a crutch because you haven't been that. When I came to see you, you were not; or at least when I was going through that period of turmoil, I was not at all aware of your actually helping me and being a support. But now that I look back on it, I might say that you have been a temporary crutch; and yet, when the wound is healed, the person is able to walk again and be free from that crutch. The wound hasn't completely healed now. . . ."

How right she was at that moment! For after that period of breakthrough, although we did not get together, she experienced intense positive and negative reactions to me and what had gone on between us. Only later when we met by chance, did I experience my ordinariness and her assuredness. What I saw in her afterward, she had expressed earlier, in the form of a declaration of intention and hope more than as an already achieved actuality: "You have really put me completely on my own. And yet—I don't feel, I really don't—I feel free from you and yet I feel closer to you than to others. That sounds strange, I know, but it's true."

The confirmation of new life comes through standing on one's own feet in one's own situation with one's own inner strength, which, of course, is both one's own and yet not one's own. Once paths have crossed, paths must separate.

Ultimate growth requires moving away from a possessive relationship with others. We prepare the way; we are not the way. That intended movement apart cannot be taken lightly. We need to ask quite realistically:

AM I HUMBLE ENOUGH for a growth relationship?

Can I really free others from my own needs so that they may unfold their own lives in their own way?

Can I really allow others to be who they are?

Can I let others become what they choose to become?

Can I be for others in ways that build them up instead of weaken them?

Am I prepared to limit my humanness in order to liberate their humanness?

Perhaps you remember that experience which Lewis Carroll describes in *Alice's Adventures in Wonderland:*

Just at this moment when Alice felt a very curious sensation, which puzzled her a good deal until she made out what it was: she was beginning to grow larger again, and she thought at first she would get up and leave the court. On second thoughts, she decided to remain where she was as long as there was room for her.

"I wish you wouldn't squeeze so," said the Dormouse, who was sitting next to her. "I can hardly breathe."

"I can't help it," said Alice very meekly, "I'm growing."

"You've no right to grow *here*," said the Dormouse.

"Don't talk nonsense," said Alice more boldly: "you know you're growing too."

"Yes, but *I* grow at a reasonable pace," said the Dormouse, "not in that ridiculous fashion." And he got up very sulkily and crossed over to the other side of the court.[21]

When we enter into a relationship, whether as a minister, a teacher, a parent, a counselor, or simply a human being, we can expect both of us to grow. We move toward each other; we move against each other; we move apart from each other. By such movements growth comes. Yet growth crowds us both. Our growth may be at a reasonable pace; the other's growth may be at an accelerated pace. When paths intersect, we can never predict how life will move. Thank God!

Six

Torn Up yet Tying Together

"I'm never going back to that church again!"

An irate mother let a greeter at the entrance to the sanctuary know how incensed she felt.

"Nor am I going to allow my children to go!"

With a jerk of her shoulders she proceeded to stamp out of the building at the close of a worship service one Sunday during Lent.

The Problem

What had happened? What could I have said to have triggered such fury? Was her response simply that of a negative, disgruntled individual and therefore something that we could dismiss as unimportant and passing? Whatever had triggered the reaction, she definitely was moving away from the congregation in a way quite contrary to the movement apart from one another necessary for growth. Here was a move against a situation that precluded contact and thereby fostered bitterness.

As events unfolded, the only unique part of the woman's comment was its vehemence. For she was not alone in being upset. Around the community, people conversed uncomfortably about the sermon. Feelings rose so high that key church leaders grew concerned. Without my knowledge, a decision was made

that the issue be discussed at the next meeting of the board of
deacons and deaconesses.

Then the chairman of that board sat down to talk with me
about people's concern. I immediately urged him to bring the
matter into the open so that everyone could be part of the
discussion, for the ministry of the Word, as well as the total
ministry of the church, was the responsibility of the entire
congregation. *They* were "the people of God" and the
ordained clergyman was not functioning as an isolated individual.
I regretted that people felt as torn up as the report indicated;
that had not been my intention nor had I anticipated the depth
and range of the reaction.

But what a marvelous opportunity!

People were involved in the meaning of ministry by virtue
of their emotional investment, even if that emotion was negative
rather than positive. I was thrilled that the chairman had already
set the process of discussion in motion. What more could a
minister ask of his people!

What had I said to provoke such turmoil?

Usually, sermon after sermon flows by causing scarcely a
ripple of response. I had not urged the recognition of Red China
by the United States, which was a red-hot issue at the time.
I had not attacked the drinking mores of the congregation,
which were fairly strict at the time. I had not pressed serious and
responsible integration, for which on another occasion I was
informed I had better start wearing a bulletproof vest. The social
polarization of the late 1960's and the beginning of the 1970's
had not yet crystallized. Our congregation tended to be broad-
minded and tolerant about controversial issues. If general
community issues were not involved, what was?

I had dealt with something more personal and intimate. I had
preached on "Sex, Sanctity, and Marriage." In the Lenten
series that year I had concentrated on The First Letter of Paul
to the Corinthians. The particular message offered on that Sunday
had attempted to examine what Paul had said and to relate it
to this crucial area of human experience.

Preparation for the Board Meeting

The time for the scheduled board meeting arrived.

Everyone knew the agenda. Copies of the sermon had been

mimeographed and distributed via the literature tables on the
Sunday prior to the meeting. Several deacons and deaconesses
had canvassed congregational opinion to get as representative
a reaction as possible. The chairman opened the meeting by
stating briefly the background of the discussion: several of the
congregation had been upset by the minister's sermon; it was felt
that the best way to deal with the situation was to have the
group directly responsible for the spiritual life of the church
explore it together.

Those who had sought a sample of opinions reported their
impressions. A small group strongly resented the fact that sex
had been dealt with from the pulpit. The woman who had
stamped out of the sanctuary was definitely estranged from
the church, at least for the present. Others, who knew from
publicity what the sermon was to be that morning, had attended
another church. A father of a fourteen-year-old girl had expressed
how uncomfortable and embarrassed he had felt sitting beside
her during the service. Several thought that the sermon would
have been all right if certain graphic words had not been used;
for example, "sex" (36 times), "sexual" (10 times), "intercourse"
(1 time), "physical intercourse" (1 time), and "sensual" or
"sensuality" (8 times). If more discretion had been used in the
choice of vocabulary, people might not have been so upset.
Some believed that the minister should deal with sexual matters,
especially with young married couples and teenagers, but not
in a morning service. One person of a liturgical bent was highly
offended that the minister had chosen Passion Sunday as the
occasion to talk about sex.

Most of the criticism came from older members. Even so,
there were a few younger members and some college students
who also felt offended. A fair-sized group expressed slight
surprise that the subject was discussed from the pulpit in such
an open manner, but they thought little more about it than that.
However, the majority, although not an overwhelming majority,
voiced appreciation. These people, by and large, were younger
and middle-aged couples, as well as college students and teenagers.
Several couples had indicated that they had been able to talk
together about their attitudes toward sex in their marriage in a
way that they had not previously, because the sermon opened the
way for them.

Freedom of the Pulpit

With those reactions before them the group itself picked up the issue.

Immediately some declared that the freedom of the pulpit must not be infringed upon. Except for perhaps one or two members of the board, the discussion was intended for sharing, not censoring. One man felt they had no business whatever even talking about the matter. The minister was the preacher; he should not have to be "called on the carpet" for what he had done. In line with this generalized halo response to authority, others indicated that in calling a minister they were placing their confidence in him as a responsible person and, therefore, such a session had no place.

Their concern for the freedom *and* responsibility of the pulpit was gratifying. Such freedom and responsibility provide a climate of expectation that encourages solid preaching. Yet such uncritical acceptance of leadership could not be allowed to distract the group from exploring together the preaching responsibility in that particular situation or in the ongoing ministry of preaching.

No minister can stand in the pulpit as a private prophet, parading his own pet prejudices. Every minister stands in the pulpit as the representative of God to the congregation and as representative of the congregation to God. Because preaching is a corporate act, the discussion by the board was most appropriate. Ideally, such discussion ought to be an ongoing process. The outbreak of upset provided the opportunity for the deacons and deaconesses to do the very thing for which they shared the responsibility with the minister.

Once the issue of legitimate, responsible, and welcomed discussion was put on the table, the exploration could continue.

Testimony

In contrast to the father of the fourteen-year-old girl, a mother of a fourteen-year-old boy expressed her pride in being in church with her son on that Sunday. Afterward, she had used the sermon as a way of talking with him about this sensitive subject.

A father spoke up: "As you know, in our family we have four boys. And when you have four boys, you can't avoid the subject of sex. Only the week before the sermon, we had had to have a talk with them on some of the physical aspects of sex. I was glad to have the subject put in its spiritual dimension within the next week. It somehow put the whole thing in the right perspective."

The anatomy professor at the university reported that he dealt with sex in his classes all the time. In fact, he could not teach his courses without dealing with sex—charts and all! He felt that sex should be discussed every year.

A college student, who served on the board as a regular member, expressed surprise at the negative reaction. He indicated that students were very free, sometimes too free, in their dealing with sex. Speaking for himself, he said that he and his fiancée had found it helpful to have worshiped together that Sunday, as did many students with whom he had talked.

A mother of four daughters, the oldest of whom was in eighth grade, had been in church with them that Sunday. Naturally, she commented, she had wondered how they had taken the sermon. At the dinner table she had asked if they had understood what the sermon had been about. Oh, yes, they had. Then, wondering what specific impressions they had carried away, she asked, "What was it that Mr. Ashbrook was getting at?" To which came the reply from her sixth grader, "He was telling us to keep our bodies clean and holy because they are the temples of God."

An unmarried person pointed out that the predicament of the single person had also been opened up in a sensitive and helpful way.

A woman responsible for teaching hygiene in the high school requested forty copies of the sermon to use as an introduction to the area of sex education with her students.

A few board members shared their own uneasiness yet gratitude that the subject could be brought within the setting of worship. Somehow it made worship more related to life and made life, especially sex, more related to worship.

By that point in the discussion the consensus of opinion had moved decisively from apprehension to appreciation.

During those first forty minutes I had refrained from comment. It was important for as many people to speak and as much to be said as possible. Any remarks by me would have tended to dampen the process. Then the chairman asked me if there was anything I wanted to say.

Of course there was!

I had a lot to say! I was excited! What a beautiful chance to lay before them the way in which I worked to tie ministry together! What a teaching opportunity! What a facilitating experience!

Using Upset for Educating

I gratefully acknowledged their willingness to engage in such free and frank discussion. If we could not talk here, where could we talk? If people could not feel free to speak the truth in love within the church, as Paul put it in Ephesians 4:15, 25, where could they be free? The discussion represented a step in the direction of transforming preaching from simply a ministerial responsibility into more of a congregational responsibility. What a crucial thing we were doing!

I expressed concern that the minority not be pushed aside in the face of general approval. Their feelings were important. What they thought needed to be both accepted *and* respected. The discussion itself reflected the board's desire to take people's opinions seriously. In agreeing upon a direction, however, we need to be as inclusive and as sensitive as possible.

With the background of openness underscored, I seized the opportunity to explain my approach to ministry. I was using one aspect of the pastoral office to describe what I was about. I might have drawn upon the counseling ministry or the organizing ministry or the shepherding ministry, but I did not. Instead, the torn-up situation provided the occasion for viewing ministry as a whole through the lens of communicating.

I am a planner—at least, of sorts. The world continually bombards us with demands. Do this! Do that! This must be taken care of *now!* Interruptions, trivia, emergencies, the unexpected come inevitably and often. Unless one takes a hand in shaping his existence, he is molded by the environment. Without long-range thinking, one reels under the impact of constant immediacy. It is emphatically so with preaching.

I planned sermon themes and worship services six months at a time. Such a process enabled me to give direction and breadth to what we shared and celebrated. For me, Lent provided an opportunity to do a heavier job of educating in the meaning of the Christian faith. I have dealt with books of the Bible, with decisive battles of the faith, and with significant spiritual leaders, among many series. In preparation for the sermons during Lent, I would decide upon a general area during the preceding summer, and work out details during the Christmas holidays. That year, I had chosen to concentrate upon a single book, The First Letter of Paul to the Corinthians. I reminded them that in the previous year's Lenten sermons I had covered the biblical witness by considering seven books, ranging from Genesis to Revelation.

In trying to understand Paul's message in First Corinthians, the whole area of sex, marriage, and sanctity had emerged. It became one of seven themes with which I had to wrestle if I were to deal with the message of the book. To explore the subject of sex in this way made it natural and appropriate, despite people's reactions. It would be just as natural and appropriate as preaching on the seventh commandment in a series on the Ten Commandments. For me to have preached on sex as an isolated topic could easily have justified the reaction, "Well, what's the matter with him? Why is he preaching on that? Does he have a hang-up over sex?" For me to deal with sex within the framework of a series on First Corinthians made it unavoidable *and* proper.

More significant than the specific subject was the preaching process. In an attempt to make the preaching ministry congregational, I had asked two groups, one made up of nine college students and the other composed of seven couples, to study the book with me in preparation for the series. From September through Lent they had tackled the material with the understanding that their discussions were feeding into the background material to be drawn together for each sermon. In that way, the sermons represented more than the minister himself wrestling with the Word; they also represented the congregation wrestling with the Word.

As the board meeting drew to a close, we experienced a deep sense of togetherness. Voicing the sentiments of others, the chairman said, "I personally feel, and I know the rest of you feel, that this has been a religious experience. And I, for one, have gotten a new insight into what goes on behind the scenes in preaching." Others spoke in a similar vein.

Then concern arose for those who had not shared in the

experience. How might the process, which the twenty-two people present had been through, be communicated? Each person took upon himself or herself the responsibility to tell others of what had taken place. Because the group was representative, they hoped the word would be passed to a large percentage of the congregation.

Reflections

Several issues took on clarity from the turmoil:

1. The subject of sex frightens and fascinates most people. The student fellowship group put aside its announced topic on the day upon which the sermon was preached to pick up questions raised by it. I was invited to speak to a personal philosophy group at the university on the subject "A Modern Realistic Christian View of Sex." When I was invited, I was told to expect a group of not more than eight or nine and that the meeting would run from eight to nine o'clock in the evening. Forty-five students showed up. After the meeting, there were further informal discussions. It was brought out that whenever there were casual conversations and counseling sessions, difficulties in the area of sex came up more often than any other topic. Subsequent experience and events have corroborated that earlier impression of the frightening and fascinating aspects of the subject.

2. Most church members genuinely want to protect the freedom of the pulpit. While all kinds of congregational and community concerns need to be taken into account, the minister must be free from pressure in order to preach the Word to the best of his understanding. In no intended way must that be compromised.

3. The preaching ministry, like all aspects of ministry, is neither exclusively nor appropriately the responsibility of the ordained clergyman by himself. It is a congregational task in its planning, in its preparation, in its presentation, in its follow-up, and in its evaluation. To the extent that it lifts up shared experience and shared direction, preaching proclaims the faith and the faithfulness of the community.

Beyond these issues, however, one issue stands out as most crucial of all. Upset provides one of the most pregnant opportunities for ministry. When faced, it activates growth. Turmoil can be the way to tie together what one is about. Criticism gives us the wedge to pry open the closed and rusty doors of communication. Contact prepares the way for communion. The separate pieces come together in a meaningful whole.

Church people, particularly, have difficulty in handling conflict. Middle- and upper-class cultures have tended to buy ease at the price of superficiality. To be nice has meant to be nonaggressive, quiet, dignified, and controlled. Cries of hurt and calls for help have gone unexpressed and unnoticed. People have maintained a distance from their differences either by talking only with those like themselves or by pulling out of stressful situations.

Not surprisingly, empirical evidence shows "a pervasive and repeated pattern of passively aggressive behavior" among church members, such as that irate woman demonstrated.[1] Such a pattern results in low morale and a chronic mild depression. This inhibition of directly moving against others means that church life tends to deny both reality and central aspects of people's personalities.[2]

In contrast, the way the sermon upset was handled suggested a moving toward each other by means of a moving against each other. By facing the growing pains of differences, the congregation did not remain childish and undeveloped. Only by remaining uncommitted do we restrict relationships to unimportant consequences, thereby robbing them of productivity and reproductivity.[3]

The preacher and the congregation learned that it was all right to look at the forbidden and the uncomfortable. The preacher and the congregation learned that friction is essential to life. The preacher and the congregation began to lose their fear of facing hurts and conflict and contrast and hope and humanness.

When the situation began to be torn up, then—although not only then—did we experience how genuinely whole we were.

Seven

Freeing the Free Ones
Administratively

The experience of grappling with a situation that upsets a congregation releases a powerful possibility. For within and beyond the particular circumstance I find an unanticipated implication:

> *The running of a church program can provide the minister with one of his most fertile opportunities for exercising pastoral sensitivity.*
>
> *Being part of such a program can give the parishioner a truly growing experience.*

Reports of ministerial perplexity and frustration tend to focus on the minister as the leader of an organization. He feels buried in "administrivia." Only with reluctance, and more often with resentment, does he divert time and energy to such tasks as budgets, bulletins, committees, and calling. He chafes under the pressure to produce institutional results.

Similarly, despite the theological claims of the church, lay people respond to the church "primarily at a socio-emotional level and not at a theological one. Their response is in terms of the organizational impact which they experience." [1] Many parishioners have a sense of being "taken" and coerced. They feel pressured to carry responsibility and they tend to take such responsibility reluctantly.

There is a layman, nearing retirement, who said, "I have always loved my church. . . . There is not one major committee in the church on which I have not served. . . . Always the relations with my minister were along the lines of church organization. But once —just once before I die—I would like to sit down with my minister and my church friends and think about ways whereby my religion could become a way of life." [2]

Or another layman confessed, "Since I joined the church, I have given most of my free time to it and frankly I have not grown in my Christian life at all. I am so bogged down in methods and in mastering the procedures that I am missing what it is all about."

This stagnant and stunting experience of "churchification" can be transformed into a healing and growing experience of humanization, for the church came into being as the people who were called out of all nations—*ecclesia*—to become "the free ones"—*eleutheroi.* "Freed from the powers of evil, the demonic powers, they now formed the free ones in . . . the assembly of God." [3]

But the question is: How? How can either the turmoil or the tedium of structure turn into transformation of spirit?

Implicit in what I have been expounding lies embedded an explicit philosophy of ministerial leadership. While this philosophy can in no way be claimed to be uniquely my own, I have arrived at it and made it mine by assimilating my experience/reflection and the reflection/experience of others. I am sure that it touches upon and expresses much that others have thought and tried to do. It does not guarantee life, but it makes life more likely.

PHILOSOPHY OF LEADERSHIP

The real life of the Spirit appears in interpersonal relationships. Where these are blocked, either between individuals or within a group, freedom and creativity are blocked. As ministers, our primary concern lies with people. In everything that we do we are to try to free these freed ones to be for others and with others and against others and apart from others as Christ was.

Relationships

To begin with, I have learned that who and what I am as a person is crucial. More important than any techniques of administration is my "person"—the atmosphere that I unconsciously create in a way that no procedure ever can. My style or image or tone—call it what you will—gives rise to a climate of expectation that provides the foundation upon which the organization rests and from which the congregation derives much of its vitality.

Consider what goes into that foundation apart from any specific administrative contact. Parishioners have heard their minister's basic understandings and values expressed in a variety of ways from the pulpit and through public prayers, as the woman described in chapter four, "Agony and Ecstasy in the Parish Context." They know how he has related to individuals in dozens of situations.

He has called in their homes, learning of their interests, their needs, their heartaches, and their hopes. He has sat with them in the hospital while minutes dragged into hours as a loved one underwent a serious operation. He has stood beside them at a freshly dug grave and shared their loneliness and emptiness with them during the ensuing months. He has rejoiced with them at family accomplishments and in family celebrations. He has come in the middle of the night in response to a frantic phone call. He has lifted their needs and his skill to God in moments of private meditation and prayer.

These, and more, flow into the unspoken dynamics present in their relationship as they make contact for organizational purposes. The quality of their relationship elsewhere sets the stage for their working relationship organizationally.

Research in the field of leadership has shown that the relationship between the members of a group and the leader of the group is the most crucial factor in determining the leader's influence over the group. Where these are warm, trusting, and admiring, morale tends to be high. Regardless of his power position the leader can affect what a group does. More of his acts will be accepted or successful although they may or may not be effective.[4]

Perhaps the subtlest aspect of minister-parishioner interaction is in the area of authority. Here is the point of greatest danger and greatest opportunity. How a member has related to other authority figures, from father to employer, is carried over and transferred to the minister. The pattern may be rebelliousness, self-effacing submissiveness, ingratiating conformity, bland agreeableness, supportive cooperativeness, collaborative responsibility, or competitive rejection. Usually, the pattern and feelings tend to be mixed.

Resistance to or acceptance of a proposed action often can be traced to disturbed relationships elsewhere. We ministers are inclined to resent the rebellious and to encourage the acquiescent. Yet it is just as damaging to encourage infantile dependency as it is to reject the active revolutionary or the persistent objector.

While a minister may occasionally be excluded from decision making, the usual pattern places him at the center of it. Members depend on him for the last word about almost everything. From the setting of a most insignificant date to whether or not a whole program should go, they turn to him for answers. Even those who exercise responsibility in their jobs tend to treat him as the all-knowing, all-wise, all-powerful father figure. If he falls into the trap of perpetuating the parishioners' feelings of personal inadequacy, the program collapses when he leaves the church, for then it will have become simply a reflection of himself rather than an expression of freed people.

Depth psychology has taught us that dependent people resent their dependency. Although this resentment may be deeply repressed, it is nevertheless present. As human beings we cannot give up our capacity for self-direction, voluntarily or under coercion, without feeling frustrated and angry.

The parishioner may consciously desire the minister to dictate policy and program; yet on a deeper level he resents such suppression of the image of God in him. Consequently, the elaborate program fails to come off. People take part hesitantly and reluctantly. They come late and leave early. They forget items of importance. They constantly put obstacles in the way of completion. Or they passively sit back and force the minister to assume all the responsibility. They convey the attitude "We will come but you do all the work." Behind the detached expression lurks the feeling "I will participate because I do not dare to displease you, but I will withhold as much of myself as possible."

To offset such a prospect and to foster a sense of corporate responsibility, the minister can continually alter the negative transference with some comment to the effect: "Whatever the group decides is all right with me" or "What does the council feel should be done in this situation?" or "What do you see as the alternatives and their consequences to the proposed action?" After a while, some people will become annoyed, but also they will begin to make decisions for themselves.

In fact, many ideas and decisions carry the group beyond anything the minister might have accomplished if he had simply stated what he thought needed to be done. For then the group would meekly accept his direction and probably fail to give the necessary support. Eventually, under such group-centered leadership, people come to the point of prefacing some discussions with, "It won't do any good to ask the minister what to do; so how does the group regard this matter?" Rather than waiting for committee chairmen to tell them what to do, they pick up the emphasis that the leader is an enabler and facilitator.

In a voluntary organization like the church, people take part on the basis of personal preference. There are no physical constraints; there are few financial returns; there are some status rewards. Thus the minister as leader has no authority and little power over the members. It is in this kind of situation where the leader has only moderate influence over the group that the relationship-oriented leader tends to perform best and be most effective.

Process

Because of the foundation of interpersonal relationships the other basic ingredient in a philosophy of ministerial leadership must be stated this way: the output is process; the program is people!

People are the aim and goal of every activity. Seldom, if ever, should people be subservient to program. The institution exists to serve persons, not persons the institution.

Consequently, programs developed apart from real and felt needs of people are of little value. Only as the members themselves participate in the conception, birth, maturation, and dying of programs do programs become meaningfully theirs.

Committee meetings, thereby, are not so much project-oriented as process-centered. Such an approach keeps the programs as the means and people as the end.

In the task of evolving program, therapeutic relationships are possible. Consider that the largest percentage of church members make up "Mr. Average Person"—the silent majority. They are clerks, secretaries, mechanics, librarians, teachers, copy readers, machinists, carpenters, salesmen, factory workers, *et al.* In the course of their day's work they have little opportunity to express their own deeply felt opinions where they count. Generally, orders come down from the top without regard to their feelings and attitudes. If they serve the public, they are subject to abuse with no outlet for pent-up emotion. Week in and week out they must listen to and do what others demand.

But when they come to church committee meetings, they find themselves in the driver's seat. No longer do they have to keep their thoughts to themselves. No longer need they cater to the whims of a superior or a customer. Now they can determine what happens! Now they have the chance to run the show! Or, from a deeper perspective, now they are in a situation in which their latent creative capacities can be activated!

Thus, everyone must "speak his piece." It makes little difference whether the remarks are favorable or critical. Once everyone has spoken, the business is dispatched. If action is taken sooner, the group must eventually spend time coping with ruffled feelings. How marvelous it is that the church can be a place that frees the free people! Here is the chance for them to cease being cogs in a machine and to discover themselves as people of potential. Technocracy dwarfs them to insignificance. They experience fate taking their destiny from them. What feels like obstructionism on the part of members, therefore, may in reality be attempts of individuals to be and become persons.

Not only must everyone speak to an issue, but at times they seem to talk about everything and focus on nothing. Any and every situation provides a target for comment. Such diversion causes frustration. Yet randomness also has a place.

All of us need a place and a relationship where we belong. If someone returns every evening to a one-room kitchenette apartment, he faces only an empty chair and a blank wall. Sanity requires reduction of stress and increase of satisfaction by means of shared experience. Whatever else they may be, committee meetings are oases of fellowship in deserts of loneliness for many more people than we realize. What on the surface seems a curse, on a deeper level is a balm.

I do not mean to imply that administration only deals with people's feelings. I do not mean to imply that administration is only therapeutically oriented and not task centered. That would be disastrous. Instead I want to convey a sense that any particular project is less significant to "the people of God"—the genuine community—than is *the experienced process of being summoned to responsibility and accountability.* What matters most is people discovering their capacity to be with one another and to act together.

INTERDEPENDENT RESPONSIBILITY

Instead of his being the center of the life of the church the minister ought to draw leadership from the congregation. Prefabricated, preset, ready-made programs are destructive of creativity, responsibility, and accountability of freed people. The minister's responsibility is to assist programs that emerge from the congregation.

By no means can the minister himself be passive or unproductive in the area of ideas and programming. On the other hand, his role should not be authoritarian, imposing programs in ways that violate the integrity of the members. Most churches are accustomed to having the minister draw his own blueprints. Because the church must free its free ones by being something more than the reflection of its minister, the minister must resist the role of strong man. Initiative and decisions must come less from the minister and more from the members.

This philosophy of relationship and process is not without its problems. In some ways there are more subtle difficulties. The approach moves on a deeper level than conventional administration.

The central complication arises with effecting the transition from a dependent relationship to an interdependent relationship. Members find it irritating to be placed in a position where responsibility rests upon them. There are times when the minister must decide to let a program fail rather than pick up the pieces after someone has not followed through. In the midst of such a crisis it takes real commitment to the congregational principle to see beyond immediate turmoil to deeper transformation.

Congregations can mature only if they are regarded as mature. That means taking the concept of responsibility seriously. When members learn that the minister really believes in their ability to respond and will neither cushion the pain of failure nor detract from the satisfaction of success, then they experience a rebirth of possibility.

There are times when patience runs thin as, for example, when one becomes anxious that something be accomplished at once.

There are times when a particular resistance seems like an overwhelming threat and one fears for the total situation.

At such times I am helped by remembering that the realization of the kingdom of God does not depend upon every little project or any particular person. Compulsiveness only ends in unhappiness and disillusionment. In the long run a congregational "sense of the meeting," to use the wonderful Quaker phrase, expresses more than any hurriedly thrown together and aggressively pressed decision. The minister's job as leader is to prepare the ground, to encourage openness and seriousness. It is the working of the Spirit that gives the increase.

In spite of all the education absorbed from the pulpit, in group sharing, and through interpretive articles, there come episodes of upset in every congregation. The sudden, emotional, adverse reaction to the sermon is a good example. Periodically, it is necessary to stop to reevaluate and to reeducate. No one can avoid the danger of moving too fast in our accelerating period of history. At times it may seem as though people are moving efficaciously. Then some minor issue becomes inflated into a major crisis. Resistance rears its head. The situation heats up. Such warnings must always be taken seriously. They enable us to get our bearings once again.

For the minister who sees administration as freeing the free ones, this area of responsibility provides a challenging outlet for his energies. The parishioner who shares in such a process comes to feel excitement and privilege. What so easily kills us can be the very means of revitalizing us. Strange as it may seem, the reconciliation and renewal of life with life is possible administratively!

Eight

Structuring the Spirit and Inspiriting the Structure

We live in an age of organizational revolution. There is no way to avoid structuring. From nursery school to business to government, we wrestle with organizational entanglements:

Who will do what?

When?

Where?

Under what circumstances?

With what resources?

For what purpose?

So the questions persist. So the demands recur.

The very act of carrying out organizational purposes often sabotages them in the process. Methods sometimes seem to negate the very goals we seek. Organization can and does obstruct progress.

The church is no exception. From its beginning, the church has struggled with the relation between its meaning and its means. Means have required people gathering for sharing and celebrating, and scattering for witnessing and serving. Much of the Bible describes the struggle with the organizational bind. Consider, for instance, the collapse of the old tribal confederacy under Saul and the birth of the new centralized monarchy under David. While most people assume that organization is necessary, most of them also report continual aggravation. The church as an institution has a tendency to get in the way of the church as a means of grace.

An aphorism describes the church's dilemma: "After the doxology, comes the theology, then the sociology."[1] Initially, an experience of new power or doxology expresses meaning beyond the present. Next comes the elaboration, reflection, and systematization of that event, or theology. Finally, the need to conserve and enhance the original experience requires the organization of people and resources, or sociology.[2]

In the beginning God brought order out of chaos. In our anxiousness and estrangement we humans have disrupted that ordering. Ever since, God has acted to reestablish the proper order of creation—that is, instead of using people and loving things, the proper order is that of loving people and using things.[3] The issue can never be as the anti-establishment radicals claim it to be: organization or no organization. The issue is always and ever:

What kind of organization?
What kind of structure?
The issue is ever and always:
How do we relate our ends to our means?
How do our means express our meanings?
Among the many biblical images about the forms which the free ones of God assume, two stand out: body and covenant. These dominate the New and the Old Testaments respectively. They are comprehensive and complementary. As images, they are clear in their own structures; they are capable of generating implications for further understanding. They enable us to think more systematically about how Spirit can be structured and how structure can be filled with Spirit.

THE BODY AND OUR RELATEDNESS

In Greek, two words are used for our word "body." *Sarx* refers to flesh or the whole person seen under the condition of weakness, off balance, distortion, and disorder. In contrast, *soma* refers to the whole person seen in his dynamic integration and proper orderliness under God. The word *soma* tightens the image of our relatedness into a working model from which we can derive specific ideas about how we structure and what we structure.

Paul provides the image of the body for us: "For just as in a single human body there are many limbs and organs, all with different functions, so all of us, united with Christ, form one body, serving individually as limbs and organs to one another." [4] In that descriptive image three organizational features stand out.

The Character of an Organization

Body constitutes the concrete character of an organization. Just as my personality is reflected through my body, as I have discussed in some detail in chapter three, so, too, an institution's spirit is reflected through its structure. Here is its "steady-state-of-behavior," its pattern or style which is always something more than what is said about it formally. The structure-maintaining feature of the body enables us to recognize the continuity of the organism over time.

The body structure may include such matters as a constitution and by-laws, the way furniture is arranged in a room, or who sits where. Who-makes-decisions and who-talks-with-whom-about-what-under-what-circumstances tell us about the nature of the organization. Even though an organization is always more than its basic structure per se, what that basic structure actually effects says a great deal about what the organization really is.

The Unity of an Organization

Body shows the essential unity of a living organism with its great diversity. There is a delicate balancing of act and counter act, of differentiation and integration. The difficulty of successful organ transplants, especially the heart, suggests the sensitive interdependence of the whole and its parts. Unless the separate organs function in harmony, pathology spreads and destroys.

One organizational expert has elucidated this point: "An organization," he states, "is characterized by an arrangement of parts that form a unity or whole which feeds back to help maintain the parts." [5] Each part has its own distinctiveness and its own dependency. The functioning of the body and the usefulness of the separate parts depend upon the appropriate interaction between them.

Thus, a breakdown of any single part eventually affects the whole. When the heart does not work or when the minister does not function, the organism is in trouble. A blood vessel or a sexton may function inadequately, but the consequence will be more aggravating than disastrous. Even so, unless the complication is dealt with, the entire body will eventually be crippled. Each part—church school teacher, financial secretary, trustee, deacon, organist—must function optimally over time for the sake of the total organization as well as for the sake of the individual involved.

Only in extreme crisis can the demands of the whole be allowed to weaken the contribution of the part; otherwise the part is lost and that loss undermines the whole.

Only in extreme crisis can the demands of the part be allowed to weaken the balancing of the whole; otherwise the whole is lost and that loss means the end of the part.

The holding together of the means for the sake of the meaning requires effective coordination and integration. Such an interacting interdependent system includes:

—clear communication among the parts,

—opportunity for members to influence the organization in ways appropriate to their level of experience and understanding,

—decision-making procedures that motivate members to carry out the decisions.[6]

When these aspects are present, spirit enlivens structure.

The Transformation of an Organization

A body develops not so much by mere additions as by inner transformation. Until what is taken in from the environment is broken down and transformed, it remains foreign and therefore harmful. Eating provides an immediate analogy. We bite into a piece of food, chew it, then swallow it. That which nourishes is assimilated; that which does not is eliminated. Without the chewing which breaks down and transforms the food into nutritional components, the act of eating may be useless at best or harmful at worst. In order to maintain a steady state, the organism must elaborate and change its structural features with the passage of time.[7]

Healthy growth, therefore, follows a lawful pattern. It takes into account size, shape, and function.[8] Without such patterning, addition to a group or organization means cancer. There is oversized, misshapened, and malfunctioning structure.[9]

As new members interact with old members, the character of a church changes. Their interactions revolve around contrasting expectations of what the institution can do and ought to do and what are the situational demands to which it must respond. Out of the give-and-take, modified patterns emerge which are never what the long-standing members desire nor what the newcomers demand. Yet there does come a change that maintains the basic integrity of the organization. By taking seriously the necessity for nurturing genuine difference, the organization remains open to renewal. ". . . only variety can regulate variety." [10]

As an image model, the body or *soma* sharpens the delicate interaction between the organism and its environment. A body neither merely reflects nor simply rejects its surroundings. It carries on continuous transactions with the setting. By virtue of such openness we have a living system.[11]

Even more to the point, the concept of the organization as body emphasizes the interrelationship of the parts with the whole. That is, it combines connectedness with differentiation. It sharpens the relationship part of the philosophy of ministerial leadership, the structure or being of an organization.

THE COVENANT AND OUR RESPONSIBILITY

By itself, the biological model is inadequate. It expresses the vitality of relatedness but not the intentionality of responsibility. It deals with connections but not with consciousness. It symbolizes being but not acting. For that a second image model is needed.

The idea of the covenant meets the doing aspect. Here is the interpersonal dimension—political in nature—that relates directly to the level of accountability. Through word and act, God established a binding relationship with his chosen people. Because of that covenant they have the task of making known his steadfast love and his sovereign righteousness. From the historical encounters of the appearance of the rainbow to Noah, the call of Abraham, the deliverance from Egypt, the giving of the Commandments at Sinai, the death and resurrection of Jesus as the Christ, and the promise of the New Jerusalem—the genuine community—three features stand out in terms of organizational implications. We shall name these trust and respect, responsibility, and reality limits.

Trust and Respect

Covenant expresses a binding relationship of trust and respect.

God freely enters into a relationship of genuine concern for the world. He does that by creating an elect, not an elite, people who are responsible for so penetrating humanity that all people become people. The idea of covenant opens up any binding relationship whether friendship, marriage, common causes, social groupings, political entity, or, ultimately, the Creator and his creation.

God established the covenant of trust for all time. Within that covenant are any number of derived or secondary covenants. From this point of view God may be understood as that reality which initiates and sustains covenants. While the trust relationship of responsibility does not necessarily place participants upon equal footing, nevertheless, it does disclose mutual confidence and the intention to hold life together in common bond. "I will be your God, and you shall be my people" expresses the heart of the matter. Such covenant is neither automatic nor inevitable. It comes from decision and commitment on the part of those involved.

Because of the element of trust, the idea of covenant conveys something more than a legal contract. While it is essential to spell out the details of rights and responsibilities, these follow from the commitment; they do not precede it. The Commandments are not the cause of God and his people getting together; they grow out of their having been together. The Commandments characterize the relationship that already exists.

Responsibility

The image of covenant clearly sharpens the issue of responsibility. Because of the bond of trust there is appropriate response. Each person is expected to maintain and deepen the meaning of the relationship. Each person seeks to make concrete the purpose of their coming together. In the Old Testament, responsibility denotes the chosen people making real justice, mercy, and peace; in the New Testament, responsibility means the new humanity making real forgiveness, reconciliation, and new reality.

In a marriage each partner carries out the vow to become "one flesh." To be overly specific about details undermines each one's sense of being a responsible person who cares about the other. Compulsive duties could only serve to suppress creativity and to hinder growth.

One of the most remarkable features of the Ten Commandments lies in their restricted content. Eight of them are stated in a negative form ("Thou shalt not. . . .") thereby bestowing extraordinary freedom in encouraging responsibility within the community. Far more than detailed obligations is the emphasis on the responsible person within a community of persons.

Reality Limits

The image of the covenant likewise recognizes reality limits. In the Old Testament, God judges people for their failure to exercise responsibility within the covenant relationship. That judgment comes in the form of slavery, captivity, invasion, exile, and the decay of morality and leadership within society itself. In the New Testament, God judges his people for their failure to exercise responsibility within the new creation. That which is against *agape,* intelligent, outgoing concern for the well-being of all, regardless of individual concerns, is destroyed by its own distortions. If a party to a covenant fails to fulfill his vow, he breaks the trust relationship, and the relationship disintegrates.

We see such collapse whenever more refined definitions of duties suffocate the smooth functioning of an organization. The more specific the details the more limited is the relationship. The more limited the relationship the more restricted are the possibilities. When one partner refuses to treat the other with respect and trust, the system explodes in a strike, a walkout, a riot, a separation, a divorce, or a polarization.

Whenever mistrust takes root, activity loses its effectiveness and personal dissatisfaction spreads. As more and more details of what one must do appear, the living relationship hardens into a literal formalism. That is apparent whether we look at the ritualistic legalism of Judaism, the moralistic puritanism of Protestantism, the sophisticated casuistry of Roman Catholicism, the minute specifications in labor-management contracts, or the particulars of a divorce adjustment. Responsibility shrivels into demanded duties.

Whenever trust takes root, activity becomes both effective and satisfying. The authority of facts and the law of the situation prevail so that people deal with real issues instead of disguised issues. Each partner respects the other. Suspicion and distortion fade. Everyone works for the well-being of all.

Perhaps even more to the point, the concept of the organization as a covenant emphasizes the task to be done. That is, it combines submissiveness with directedness. It sharpens the task part of the philosophy of ministerial leadership, the functioning or acting part of the organization.

CONSEQUENCES FOR A CHURCH'S BECOMING

What are the implications of the image models of a healthy body and a true covenant for Spirit and structure? How do they combine to produce a dynamic direction?

Structure Matters

Whether we like it or not, organization matters. Niebuhr's term "pastoral director" as a descriptive pattern for ministry, while not completely satisfactory, does ground us in a structure.[12] A disembodied spirit or a structureless ministry has no reality.

Ministers tend to stress meaning, but they constantly gripe about the means required to carry out the meaning. We who deal with ideas and ideals, such as education, science, creativity, freedom, trust, responsibility, integrity, and identity, often fail to recognize the dependence of these ideals upon appropriate administrative arrangements.[13] Theologically, we need to remember that God employed the structure of the world. "To save, Christ—the new Adam—had to assume precisely the form and predicament of the old Adam." [14]

Certain procedures and divisions of authority encourage covenant relationships; others hinder them. For example,

> —as groups increase in size, they decrease in intimacy. Members in smaller churches report more intense commitment than those in larger churches.[15]

The larger the group the greater the demands on the leader, the greater the group's tolerance of his direction, the more the active members dominate, the more the less active members acquiesce, the less personal the atmosphere, the longer it takes to arrive at decisions, the more acceptable are unresolved differences, the greater the number of subgroups, the more formalized the rules and procedures.[16]

> —if chairs face the chairman and if, in addition, he sits behind a large desk, contact is reduced and distance is increased. Physical obstacles act as psychological barriers.

Clearly, the issue is not, and never can be, structure or no structure. In the second century, the Montanists were only partially correct in rebelling against church organization in the name of the Spirit. They were right in emphasizing the prophetic in contrast to the priestly, expectation in contrast to establishment, and possibility in contrast to fixation. They were wrong in not seeing the necessity for structure. In fact, they rapidly fell into the pattern of every ecstatic sect. They developed a strict discipline of their own in order to insure continuity. Despite their attack, they themselves recreated a structure.[17]

We cannot avoid facing the question of how we structure Spirit.

Forms Vary

While formal structure matters, the forms of structure vary.

Articles of incorporation must be broad and durable in order to image the meaning of the organization. The activities of the Ministers and Missionaries Benefit Board of the American Baptist Convention, for instance, have ranged from pensions and emergency grants, to counseling and career development, to support of civil rights, to investment in black banks, all under the overall purpose of "the better maintenance of the ministry."

By-laws, in contrast, need to be specific and changeable in order to carry out purposes. The more rapid the acceleration in society, the more flexible the organizational structure needs to be.

For people on the move, the portable tent of the wilderness may be a more appropriate symbol than the permanent temple in the city. Except for some kind of organizing center to delegate responsibility, it may be that all committees should be *ad hoc,* created in response to special need and disbanded when the need no longer exists.

No single pattern of organization applies automatically. Sometimes an overemphasis upon group decisions works against the capacity to respond. It places a premium on "going along" or "playing the game" or being "part of the team." At other times an underemphasis upon group decisions reduces the capacity for creativity and imagination. It isolates individuals from stimulation and support. Dynamic fluidity, therefore, requires an atmosphere of adventuresomeness coupled with continuous communication.

People need encouragement to discover unsuspected ways of wedding meaning and means in changing circumstances. I am proposing an experimental approach to organization. Every situation is reexamined in light of current demands and accumulated knowledge. On the other hand, I am recommending the risk of faith as an approach. We move out, like Abraham, uncertain of where we are going and of what we will find.

The excitement of experimentation requires continuous communication among the part(ner)s. Feedback as to what is and is not happening and circulation of that information are the sharpened tools of cybernetics.[18] Ideas must flow back and forth from the youngest to the oldest, from the most marginal to the most central, from members to minister. Instead of differences destroying the unity, they serve to keep people working until a more adequate and usually unanticipated direction emerges. The tension "provides the 'go' of the system, the 'force' behind the elaboration and maintenance of structure." [19]

When communication "levels," then people know that they matter. Their reactions are taken seriously. They have a significant say in what goes. They lend a critical hand in what unfolds. Their ideas count. Differences are exchanged in an atmosphere of acceptance *and* appreciation.

People, Primary

People are the heart of every process and the meaning of every program. Individuals are seen as responsible. They are capable of initiative, imagination, judgment, and evaluation. Not only do they contribute in their own area of specialty but also in the overall activity. They are both the means and the meaning of the church becoming a genuinely *human* community.

If people are indeed primary, then we need to appreciate individual differences as well as encourage them to "be" who they are.

Each of us comes at the world with unique equipment for seeing, organizing, and evaluating the world. No two people ever encounter precisely the same situation. Individuals are, in truth, individual in their biological equipment, their social conditioning, and the integration of the two.[20] Rather than being amazed at the unpredictable range of people's reactions, we ought to be disturbed when differences fail to appear. If we ignore individuality, we miss individuals.

Research has disclosed that ministers have a distinct pattern of becoming aware of the world and of evaluating events.[21] In contrast to other academically trained groups, they tend to be more aware of people than ideas; they evaluate the world more in terms of personal warmth and feeling than impersonal logic and thinking; they prefer getting things done rather than exploring possibilities. Despite their emphasis upon meaning and values, they are inclined to handle matters in a routine manner rather than to focus on process. In short, as a group, they like to work with people and they want to see things happen.

Organizational trouble often stems from not recognizing differences in values. Research shows almost no predictable relationship between the way in which ministers evaluate the consequences of their work and the way in which parishioners evaluate those same consequences. They simply fail to see the organization in the same way.[22] Where such discrepancy reflects conflict between prophetic faith and acculturated religion, the tension is appropriate and desirable.[23] Where such dissonance stems from a breakdown in communication and shared commitment, the stress is unnecessary and destructive.

Because people are primary, we must have the courage to let them "be," even as God lets us "be." That "letting-be" implies an active, positive "enabling to be, empowering to be, or bringing into being."[24] We respect individual styles by developing the strengths of individuals. The organization thrives on, even more depends on, the variety and idiosyncrasies of its members.

Larger Purposes

A final consequence of the body-covenant image comes in knowing quite definitely that the organization does not exist as an end in itself. "People don't co-operate just to co-operate; they co-operate for substantive reasons, to achieve certain goals, and unless these are comprehended the little manipulations for morale, team spirit, and such are fruitless."[25] Being-together and letting-be must not overshadow the commitment to making known genuine humanity in genuine community.

For that larger purpose we need to establish and maintain priorities with periodic evaluation.

A major source of personal frustration may be found in feeling that we are at the mercy of an overpowering environment. We experience ourselves primarily as *reacting* to circumstances instead of *acting* by means of circumstances. Most of us do not maintain enough distance from pressures in order to sort out our priorities. Because we are unclear of what we are about, we end up being swamped by everything.

Distance comes with the first realization that only a very few demands are urgent. That telephone call can be made at 11:45 A.M. when study draws to a close, instead of at 9:15 A.M. when study should begin. That tearfully frightened woman can be scheduled at 2:00 P.M. instead of at 7:30 A.M. when she would rush over in panic. In fact, the later time enables her to anticipate the relationship and so to use it more productively; it also helps her to learn that she can live through anxiety without being destroyed.

By setting a time schedule in which each demand is given its proper place, we create a balanced program. Of course there are exceptions. Sometimes study will be disrupted by death, and counseling may be disrupted by a speaking deadline; but for about 80 percent of the time the balanced schedule works.

Nothing sharpens meaning and orders means better than periodic reflection on what takes place. True "letting-be" depends upon allowing to be present and operating what is in fact present and operating.

Evaluation pulls into the foreground dynamics that have been operating in the background. By asking:

"What's going on?"

"What's taking place?"

"I wonder how to account for what's happening?"

"How do you feel about what we're doing?"

"How might we handle this differently?"

the leader can loosen defensiveness, free resistances, examine possibilities, mobilize curiosity, and enhance commitment.[26] Such an approach gets across the message that meetings are for meeting and that programming is process.

"What's going on?" might involve simply the describing of what has transpired. Who said what to whom, and when? Who is quiet and under what circumstances? What are people saying by the way they sit and the way they gesture?

Attention might be focused on the impact that restlessness, boredom, silence, repetition, and "barking" have on the group. Connections might be made between uncertainty about someone's motives and resistance to that person's suggestions. Persistent, intense, and inappropriate responses call for an attitude of curiosity.

We try to get behind surface behavior to uncover deeper personal meanings.

A more systematic evaluation can increase members' sensitivity to what takes place in committees and groups.[27] For a group to go through such a process and then to talk about the results will invariably increase responsibility and deepen participation.

In order to structure spirit and inspire structure, the minister has to combine the task to be done with consideration of the persons involved. Roles must be defined; expectations must be explored; uncertainty must be tolerated; individuals must be free to take initiative and to express differences. When ministers are intolerant of member initiative and unskilled in defining and organizing expectations and responsibilities, the organization suffers. When ministers are sensitive to people and their interaction and are adept at getting groups and people to work, the organization comes alive.[28]

Where the courage to "let be" is present, people commonly say, "I am made to feel like a person." And increasingly they remark, "This is really a community."

responding-to-being-in-this-world

Man wishes to be confirmed
in his being by man,
and wishes to have a presence
in the being of the other
. . . .

secretly and bashfully
he watches for a Yes
which allows him to be
and which can come to him
only from one human person to another.
Martin Buber [1]

True partnership puts my mind
at the service of my partner. . . .
Our minds work much better for our
partners than for ourselves.
The Spirit was not given to man for
himself. . . .
Eugen Rosenstock Huessy [2]

Nine

Through a Glass Darkly,
but Then...

Traditional pastoral care has concerned itself with individuals in developmental and situational crises. Lately, the focus has broadened from the individual in isolation to the individual in interaction in groups. Regardless of the older cure of souls or the current concern for persons, the central emphasis remains the individual.

Parallel to preoccupation with the individual have been two contrasting and usually competing emphases. One has tended to restrict itself to the church as the body of Christ, the household of faith, the fellowship of believers; the other has tended to transcend itself in ministry to culture and society. Regardless of the differences between these two emphases, their central concern has continued to be organizational and structural.

By and large, the people in pastoral care and counseling have not learned from Marxian analysis that the structures of society cripple or cure individuals collectively. Enamored by the shepherding image of rescuing/comforting/nurturing or of the psychodynamic paradigm of analysis/insight/responsibility, they have tended to retreat from the complexities of a confusing and crushing culture into the simplistic safety of the therapeutic womb.

On the whole, pastors and activists have not learned from psychological analysis that what goes on inside a person affects what that person does and how he does it in the world. Enamored of formal institutional patterns or of informal political processes, they have tended to retreat from the muddy messiness of personal intimacy into the clear clash of power politics without regard to the individuals involved and affected.

Fortunately, the decade of the 1960's evidenced a rapprochement between care of the isolated individual and concern for the deindividualizing society.

PERSONS AND STRUCTURES

Don Browning exemplified the refocusing when he analyzed the relationship of pastoral care and public ministry to each other. He pointed out that concern with the whole gospel demands that we see "individuals against the background of the social structures" but also see "the social structure against the background of the struggle of the individual." [1]

Laboratory training in group dynamics and sensitivity reflects a similar struggle and tentative collaboration between turning inward for insight into personality factors ("the Yogi") and turning outward for social salvation within the matrix of organizational factors ("the Commissar"). The debate has been between Lewinians and Freudians, between self-actualizers and organizational improvers, between the individual as client and the organization as client.[2]

Comprehensive community mental health and antipoverty programs both reflect the tension between the dynamics of individual psychology and the dynamics of social structures; neither can be translated easily into the other's framework.[3] "What is needed is not a translation," states one community-oriented psychiatrist, "but a search for some coherent interface between individual dynamics and group or community behavior." [4]

Within this wider background the small-group process is to be emphasized as one means of establishing "some coherent interface" between individual growth and organizational change.

Group Process as Bridge

Much personal and group conflict is spawned in misunderstanding and spreads from reinforced misperceptions. Without face-to-face contact we read our fears and fantasies into one another. The check that comes with feedback is missing. Since we see each

other only through a glass darkly, we remain enigmas, riddles—
mysteries, as the Greek word in 1 Corinthians 13:12 implies.
And because of this, we drift dangerously apart.

In contrast, as we are in touch, we discover built-in correction
for our misperceptions. Mystery, uncertainty, and fearfulness re-
cede. In their stead come understanding, knowledge, and an ability
to cope with what is.

Small groups provide a tested means of fostering contact for
the purpose of affecting change. The method requires bringing
together people from diverse and often polarized backgrounds.
They find themselves in a structurally controlled setting conducive
to exposing unexamined stereotypes and, hopefully, demolishing
them. People are encouraged to share the ways in which they
see themselves and one another. It is hypothesized that the con-
frontational-encounter method increases personal awareness, modi-
fies attitudes, and improves interpersonal competence.

FORMS OF SMALL GROUPS

The small-group process has assumed a variety of forms.
Though the process can be harmful, results are constructive if it is
utilized properly.

The laboratory method, perhaps the most highly developed of
the patterns, lifts people out of their normal surroundings for
periods ranging from a few days to two or three weeks.[5] Similarly,
the marathon method confines a heterogeneous group in a room
for continuous interaction for eighteen to forty-eight hours.[6]

The strength of these approaches lies in freeing individuals of
ordinary demands and ongoing responsibilities. They experience
themselves as unique individuals interacting with other unique individuals. But this strength is also its limitation. Removed from
ongoing contexts, people experience an air of unreality. There are
no structural bridges back into the routine. The mountaintop
meeting of person with person tends to remain on the mountaintop—an episode—and does not get back into the valley.

In contrast to laboratory experiences, police in Houston meet
with militant minority members three hours once a week, for
six weeks at a time. The minority members believe that the controlled verbal confrontation enables them to get across to repre-
sentatives of the "oppressive" establishment the perilous consequences of misreading minority attitudes.[7]

Required unstructured small groups in a seminary kept students dealing with both themselves and the dynamics of the institution.[8] The same process paved the way for institutional change to take account of black students' demand for recognition (see chapter 11).

Within the church the small-group emphasis has been one of the most powerful means for renewal. By sharing and searching together, people have found solidarity and significance. They have become more themselves, more open to diversity and depth, and more able to orient their lives in terms of powerful religious meaning.

When the small-group method of personal confrontation-encounter is part of ongoing interaction, the possibilities for structural change are enhanced. Individual understanding is linked with behavioral involvement, reinforced by reality. Whether they like it or not, people have to deal with each other over a period of time. As more reality is present, more constructive and satisfying patterns emerge.

Three other applications of the method will be described in the rest of this chapter. One involves an initial experience of suburbanites and inner-city residents coming together to form a community-based organization for neighborhood change. The second suggests what can happen in a public school classroom. The third comes from the closed society of explosive Mississippi. Each uses an ongoing setting as the base for small-group contact as a means of effecting social change.

THE SMALL GROUP IN COMMUNITY ORGANIZATION

In an inner-city area a nonprofit organization is needed for neighborhood improvement. Such a corporation would serve as a vehicle for carrying out the expressed needs of the neighborhood, including the construction and rehabilitation of housing, obtaining personnel and facilities to fill the need for a variety of social services for the immediate area, and working with professional planners to obtain a feasible overall plan of action for neighborhood development. The venture would require the direct involvement of indigenous residents plus the additional talent and interest of outsiders.

How does one bring together eager suburbanites and wary inner-city residents? How can the task be accomplished?

In drawing up an agenda for an initial meeting, the community organizer, the Reverend Stanley E. Skinner, Jr., had to take into account both the political task and the people required to do the task. If the task were the sole focus, personal motivations could be misread, causing a miscarriage of the project before it was launched. If personal relationships were the sole focus, the need for change would be neglected, causing a misconception of the undertaking. Somehow the action task had to be primary, supported by reality-based understanding among those involved as to who they were and why they bothered. Some form of face-to-face methodology seemed appropriate.

The first of several organizing meetings of the new corporation was called, and twenty-three people packed a large living room in the area. There were neighborhood leaders of the local block clubs, which, in turn, were knit together in the Neighborhood Association. There were also church-related suburbanites, both Protestant and Catholic. Many were strangers—uncomfortable, awkward, wanting to help, uncertain how to gear in. The crowding of the room generated an air of excitement and expectancy. People came late; people left early; people shifted seats; people relished their refreshments; all of this disruption contributed to some confusion during the three-hour session.

For about an hour and a half, ideas tumbled out, as they brainstormed as to what was needed and how it might be accomplished. During a break for coffee and cake, Skinner, as the convener, structured what could be called the formal introduction of the two groups to each other—not as two groups but as several individuals from two distinct worlds. The following is an excerpt from a verbatim account of the interchange:

Convener: I'd like to ask the suburban people from the corporation committee to say a few words about how they became interested in the area community and their motivations for putting themselves at the disposal of the neighborhood people. Let's go right around the room.

A university professor from the Catholic group: As a teacher at the university, I can reach a lot of people with ideas, but I have few opportunities to act on what I believe in a physical sense. I feel an obligation to do those things I am usually talking about. As a Catholic layman, I feel I might be able to work in this place in this way. I admire the spunk of this community and your community loyalty. I don't see the apathy here that we've been trained to look for in the inner city. Probably it's here, but you seem to have a core of active people to work with.

An industrial engineer from the Protestant group: Well, I'm from the South. When I came to Rochester, I only had about $14 and a wife, and we lived over on East Avenue; but it wasn't a very fashionable place, up over the Studebaker garage there on East Avenue, down toward the city. And then the government built the VA housing over there and I moved in and stayed about seven years. Well, it really helped me a lot, and it was low-income housing there—the VA housing—and I guess I'd like to be part of a group that can put up some housing and stuff here in this neighborhood.

An industrial chemist from the Catholic group: I guess I'd have to agree with ______. I just feel that all my life I've been given advantages that I really didn't earn. I mean, I've worked hard, but I've had a lot of breaks. People have been there at the right times and the right places for me. I don't know; I guess I feel that the advantages I have now aren't really mine, because I didn't earn them, and I want to give others help like I got.

A woman social worker from the Catholic group: I'm working as a public health nurse, and I've heard people over here say they've needed a clinic of some sort, either diagnostic or medical—the medical's more expensive—but I'd like to help in any way I can.

An industrial planner from the Protestant group: I work over at ______. I do planning, draw up flow charts, which tell the steps in how to do something, and make presentations to boards, and things like that. I'd like to do this kind of work for you, since you're asking for professional help for your neighborhood. Also I'd just like to help.

Other persons followed with similar expressions of interest. Through their church connections in the area these suburbanites wanted to give themselves in ways which they thought were significant. When each of them had finished, Skinner continued the structured encounter.

Convener: I wonder if we can go around the room again, and maybe the neighborhood people can say how they tie into this. I mean, why are you for the corporation and how did you become interested?

A woman inspector in an optical instrument company: I'm interested in getting a PTA started here in the square. Some of us have had some trouble at the school with the kids, and I think—I don't know that the corporation will improve the whole neighborhood, but if we get a community center, then it'll give the people some place to get together and maybe we'll have some community spirit, you know. I guess that's why I got into it. One of the ministers was talking to me one day, and kind of got me interested in the whole thing.

A housewife, speaking very slowly: I don't know—I've lived here all my life, and I like it here. And if my house could be a little more livable—the landlord won't do anything now— well, then, it would be a good place to live and I'd like to stay on here.

Another woman: Well, I certainly do think it's nice of all you people to come here this way, and—I don't know, I've lived on the same street all my life. I mean, I was raised here and the people I work with have all moved out to the suburbs, and they are always saying, "Are you still living on Plymouth? Why are you still living there?" And "Aren't you afraid to walk the streets at night?"

I just say, "No. I'm not afraid to walk the streets at night and why should I be?" I mean, that's ridiculous. The people know that I belong there—I mean, on Plymouth. And so I'm not afraid to walk the streets, but these people where I work, they talk as though I'm hardly existing, you know. Like if you don't live in the suburbs, you hardly even exist. And I just think that's dumb. I mean, it's not right. I like it here, but I wish it were fixed up better and so that's how come I'm here.

Another neighborhood person breaking in: I was doing some calling on Verona Street yesterday—you know, with the sheets we're supposed to take around for the corporation thing. I only got to three houses and, at the fourth house where I went, I was talking to some people in this one apartment and then I heard some shouting from the next apartment, 'cause the door was open, and I thought, "Well, I'd better go and see if something is wrong," you know? So I went over and I says something about maybe there was some sort of crisis, you know, and whether maybe I couldn't help.

Well, it turns out that this woman was shouting at the man what could she do about the babies. She has two sick children and each of them with 104° temperature. So, as it turns out, I went home and got the car and took them down to the hospital, and so that's all the calling I did. I didn't get too many names. But we really need some sort of clinic where people can go, *locally,* you know, because this woman didn't have any car or anything.

Other neighborhood inhabitants explained similar experiences motivating their involvement in the proposed organization. They saw need—whether their own or others—and they felt that only concerted action would help.

Clearly the suburbanites came to the inner-city neighbors with a sense of obligation rising out of their own personal circumstances. Some of them had received help in the past without damage to their self-esteem. Others had personal resources which led them to be responsible individuals in all phases of their lives. Clearly, the local people wanted to be where they were, but equally they wanted better conditions. Their collaborative involvement in community organization was strengthened by the personal disclosures and sharing of those present.

Each group was able to move from only dimly seeing the other to seeing the other more directly. The personal reality strengthened the action task; the action task gave significance to the personal reality.

THE SMALL GROUP IN PUBLIC EDUCATION

The public school presents a distinct contrast to a community organization. Next to the penal system, no recipients of an institution's service have less say over whether they will participate or how they will participate than elementary and secondary school pupils. Today the schools have become the focal point for the most intense efforts at effecting *or* resisting social change. Historically, public education has provided the foundation for political democracy and upward mobility. Currently, unless quality integrated education succeeds, American democracy will not survive.

The impact of much education tends to be failure-oriented. Regardless of reasons for the failure, recommendations for change are going to come primarily within the existing framework. Despite exciting experimental programs, broad-based, tax-supported, community-accepted programs are still the structures with which we will have to work.

One program that is producing change within the existing framework is that developed by William Glasser, a psychiatric consultant with the Los Angeles City and Palo Alto Schools. The approach emphasizes the basic relationship between people, the reality demands of the situation, the exercising of responsibility in adapting to those demands and the self-respect that stems from behaving in a manner that allows everyone to experience satisfaction and fulfillment. Relatedness plus reality plus responsibility plus self-respect equal meaningful living. Such is the philosophy behind reality therapy.[9]

More specifically, the principles of reality therapy as applied to schools without failure are based on the assumptions that:

1. The first years of school are critical for success or failure;
2. Many children bring a loneliness to school that leads to failure;
3. Unless a pupil in some way first experiences success in one important area of his life, he will not succeed in life generally.

Glasser takes these assumptions and translates them into an educational philosophy that requires:

1. The acceptance of all pupils as potentially capable and not as handicapped by their environment;
2. The elimination of failure;
3. The importance of thinking beyond simply memorizing;
4. The teaching of relevant issues itself as part of the educational process—that is, stating relevant problems, finding reasonable alternatives, and implementing what seems to be the best alternatives.

The approach requires that a school adopt such procedures as classes grouped only by age, the abolishing of letter grades for a pass-superior or no failure system, and classroom discussion meetings.[10]

It is the use of the small-group classroom method that is of immediate concern. Glasser has pupils place their chairs in a

tight circle so that no one is either in front or back. The teacher
or leader sits in a different place for each discussion. Pupils,
especially in the elementary grades, must raise their hands and be
recognized before speaking. Mutual listening and mutual involvement are thereby encouraged.[11]

These circle discussions are of three kinds:

1. Social-problem solving. *"All problems relevant to the class
as a group and to any individual in the class are eligible for discussion."* [12] The discussion is always directed toward solving the
problem without finding fault.

2. Open-end. Any thought-provoking question related to the
lives and interests of the pupils.

3. Educational-diagnostic. The pupils voice their opinions and
conclusions about the curriculum.[13]

The meetings come just before dismissal and run from ten to
fifteen minutes in the primary grades and up to twenty-five or
thirty minutes in the secondary grades.

After extended conversations with the Department of Pupil Personnel Services of the Rochester City Board of Education and
after presenting the program to an elementary school faculty, I
began meeting with a second-grade class in January, 1970, using
the classroom discussion circle. The teacher, Miss June Chisholm,
worked with an extremely difficult class, primarily because seven
of her twenty-six children exhibited definite behavior problems.

"After having tried every technique and method at my com-
mand for reaching my class of 'losers,' " she commented at the
end of the year, "I was, in a way, grasping at another straw when
I decided to try Dr. Glasser's plan."

For five months five days a week the children talked.

As they talked, *they looked at problems:* throwing snowballs,
talking after the bell rings, losing pencils, "love" notes, "hate"
notes, report cards, not wanting to be in the circle, lunchroom
behavior. *They described their interests:* monsters, horses, model
cars, superheroes, more monsters, the circus, spring, Easter,
more monsters. *They struggled with "thought" topics:* suppose
you had no eyes, what would you do? Suppose you woke up
tomorrow and all the boys were girls and all the girls were boys,
what would you do? Suppose someone gave the class two airplane
tickets to fly to Washington to see the President for a day,
how would we decide who would go? *They evaluated their lessons:*

why do we bother studying phonics? What good is arithmetic? Does it matter whether you know how to read? How would you teach next year's second-grade class to read?

Miss Chisholm described some of the initial problems:

> Children were hesitant to talk since they were geared to the old teacher-directed methods.
>
> "I was very nervous and insecure about what topics should be chosen, how to direct discussion, what comments, if any, to make, what reactions, if any, to show, and how to pull it all together at the close of each session."
>
> Setting up a routine with definite rules and holding to it;
>
> Being able to accept *anything* said, without making any verbal judgments;
>
> Not requiring everyone to speak;
>
> Realizing the new "freedom" would release words *and* actions.

"I wondered at first," Miss Chisholm continued, "and felt some feelings of guilt at daily using this time which would have been used for regular lessons. But soon I began to feel that the marked improvement, not only in behavior and attitude, but also in achievement, made the time well-spent."

Let me describe some of the changes in terms of specific children. I have given them fictitious names.

When the circle started, Peter was knocking over desks, kicking chairs, and banging people. He could not sit still. His comments tended to be extraneous and disruptive. Several times he had to be removed from the circle. By the thirteenth week, Miss Chisholm spontaneously observed, "My word! Peter's really thinking! He used to just fool around. Now he's listening and his responses are thoughtful."

When I first entered the classroom, Harriet sat at her desk pushed back into a corner, with her thumb in her mouth. By the fourth week, her behavior took a sharp shift that left the teacher feeling bewildered and defeated at first. Harriet went on a "hate" campaign against Miss Chisholm. By the ninth week, she began to respond to suggestions without resistance or resentment. By the eleventh week, she exchanged desks with another pupil in order to be next to the teacher. By the thirteenth week, she badgered the other children and would rebel at times when asked to do something. By the end of the year she had volunteered a comment in reading class, she had spoken in the circle, she was playfully alive with her peers, and she would look in the window after school just to smile at the teacher!

Perhaps the most dramatic change came in Jonathan, a slow, possibly brain-damaged, child. Before the circle started, he said little. When he did say anything, his mumbling was hard to understand. As the weeks passed, Jonathan took an increasingly active part in discussions. His observations were sensible and to the point. Whereas the group at first grudgingly put up with his stumbling efforts, eventually they came to listen with respect.

The turning point came in a discussion of superheroes. Henry, the brightest one in the class, assumed the lead. He confidently declared that a superhero was one who flies. Deliberately leaning forward on his chair, his arms firmly planted on his thighs, with his hands folded, Jonathan declared, "I disagree with you! Batman doesn't fly and he's a superhero."

Henry sat back somewhat taken aback. After about a minute and a half he announced, "I was wrong."

Since then, the two have agreed *and* disagreed on matters of opinion. In one discussion someone was disagreeing with Henry about where the motor was in a certain car. Finally, to settle the argument, Henry turned to Jonathan for the last word. In the election of officers in the social studies class in the thirteenth week, Jonathan was elected vice-president of his section. He even wrote a platform speech despite the difficulty he had putting ideas into words, let alone on paper.

The changes between January and June were dramatic, even though from day to day or week to week not much seemed to be happening. Some topics fell apart in discussion. Other sessions became so disrupted that they had to be stopped, but always with the idea "we will try again tomorrow." Miss Chisholm's list of progress included:

gradually less horseplay and attention-seeking devices;
a greater interest in talking and staying on the subject;
more thoughtful suggestions;
better recognition of problems;
better understanding of the children's "hang-ups" by herself; and

a more honest and accepting picture of the teacher by the children.

My list of progress included aggressive behavior more controlled; restless activity reduced; withdrawnness modified; self-image improved; the teacher's understanding more of what goes on between herself and the pupils as well as how the way they view themselves affects what they do; a reduction of the gap between the class and non-class experiences; the group's dealing with discipline as a problem-solving task; and the development of the pupils' ability to think and evaluate for themselves.

"This has given me a purpose in my teaching," Miss Chisholm commented late in the spring. "I had lost it. Now I'm seeing that teaching involves much more than simply reading, spelling, writing, and arithmetic."

She has talked with her colleagues of her experience. We have presented it to her faculty. With the backing of the Pupil Personnel Services staff and the contagion of change we agreed to try the method in sixteen classes in two different elementary schools during the next school year. As the climate of the classroom changes, the possibilities for the pupils multiply.

THE SMALL GROUP IN A STATE COUNCIL ON HUMAN RELATIONS

Since 1965, Kenneth Dean has served as executive director of the Mississippi Council on Human Relations. In the arena of racial conflict the assignment has proven central and sensitive. He has applied the small-group confrontational model in a variety of forms. Three illustrations suggest its flexibility.

Early in 1965, while Dean was attending a Civil Rights Commission hearing in Jackson, a white Roman Catholic businessman approached him. The man owned two dairies, one in southern Mississippi and one in the central region. The southern plant was being boycotted by the Klan because he was a Catholic, while the other was being boycotted by the blacks because of his employment policies. He sought help for the latter boycott. He did not consider himself a strong racist, but he did belong to the White Citizens' Council. He was an active leader in church and in the community.

After reviewing the situation with the black community and a number of white businessmen, Dean learned that still another boycott had been organized by the White Citizens' Council against any white businessman who did not join the council or who did not display the council's seal on the window of his place of business. Written in red, white, and blue, the seal read, "States' Rights and Racial Integrity."

Upon reporting that to the dairy owner, Dean was invited to meet with the Citizens' Council to discuss the issue. He was surprised to find the council meeting in the city hall and, along with three or four leading businessmen, the officers of the council consisted of city and county-elected public officials.

He set as his goal the dissolving of the White Citizens Council, utilizing small-group confrontation. At the time, the black boycott was having considerable effect. Because of the squeeze, the council agreed to meet with Dean each Wednesday evening for a two-hour period. About fourteen men attended.

The meetings began with a discussion of how each felt toward the boycott. That led to how each felt about blacks in general. Dean would role-play a black leader confronting them with the issues. From time to time members broke into shouting rages; some walked out. At other times they pulled off their coats, rolled up their sleeves, screamed and cursed at Dean, inviting him and his "nigger friends" to a street fight.

Over a period of six weeks, four men dropped out, stating that they could not stand up under the process. Dean continued meeting with the rest of them for about six months. At the end of that period, they agreed on the following plan. Six of the remaining ten consented to sit down with six leaders chosen from the black community. The group met twice. Then it divided into three smaller groups of two blacks and two whites each.

Considerable community change resulted. The six who stayed in the process largely facilitated the developments. Not to be minimized, however, was the fact that some who dropped out of the group stopped advocating violence, whereas previously they had advocated violent resistance. They were not involved in biracial activity, but only on rare occasions did they block new efforts at social change.

Eventually the dairyman lost his business. With a bank loan he started a tire shop. In 1969, he was serving as president of the Chamber of Commerce. Recently he approved the applications of seven Negro businessmen for membership in the chamber. He supports the antipoverty program and participates in programs of social justice in the Catholic church.

In reflecting upon the change, Dean believes that through the small-group confrontational process a number of men were able to surface their anxieties and prejudices. After gaining courage to talk about these among their peers, they no longer needed to feed upon the problems of race. Those who withdrew faded into the background and were no longer considered to be community leaders. Those who continued developed personal strength that allowed them to reorient their leadership attitudes to include blacks. They are able to communicate across racial lines and to discuss publicly a new position regarding race. The White Citizens' Council has disbanded. The seals have been removed.

While not personally responsible for the following activity, Dean observed it firsthand and reported it to me. The Student Nonviolent Coordinating Committee movement of 1964, 1965, and 1966 was based upon the belief that great resources of intellectual and leadership ability lay dormant in the black people of the Delta. These abilities, it was believed, could be called forth through the careful structuring of personal relationships coupled with frequent mass meetings. Potential black leaders were singled out and civil rights volunteers trained to enter into personal relationships with these leaders. In many instances the civil rights volunteers lived in the homes of the prospective leaders. Their task was primarily that of listening to the blacks.

About twice a week mass community meetings were held. They had the twofold purpose of informing people of current developments and providing a chance to express needs and complaints. They usually lasted about four and a half hours. In the meeting, potential leaders were encouraged to take an active part. Civil rights advocates usually described the meeting format as that of "a radical democracy," an effort aimed at generating consensus.

Robert Moses (now Robert Parrish) shared in the development of this approach to the creation of black community leaders. In conversation with Dean he described how he was influenced by Paul Tillich's *Love, Power and Justice,* supplemented by his reading of Albert Camus and Carl Rogers. Moses' role in the movement included the training of civil rights volunteers and Student Nonviolent Coordinating Committee workers in group dynamics, influenced by Rogers' emphasis upon the possibilities of change through the careful structuring of personal relationships. It needs to be noted that this process developed in conjunction with the group process of the mass meeting.

Since 1966, Dean has worked with War on Poverty personnel. Most staff persons, both black and white and both professional and subprofessional, approach the problems of poverty with an emphasis upon physical surroundings and systems instead of attempting to understand the nature of persons. Translated into programs the inevitable suggested solution for poverty is a bulldozer to tear down slum dwellings or a bucket of whitewash and a bar of soap.

In training these workers, Dean usually concentrates upon groups of about fifteen. He begins by asking each participant individually, "Describe the kind of person you dislike most." That is followed by the question, "What kind of person do you like most?" After about an hour's exploration participants usually recognize that they do not like poor people. Racial prejudices on the part of both black and white appear as a byproduct of the process. By the end of a three- to four-hour session, most workers readily admit that they do not like the poor and that they do have racial prejudices.

With that awareness, Dean then raises the question: "How do you expect to work with people whom you do not like?"

In the second training session Dean gives a brief statement on "what a person is." He uses Rudolf Bultmann's material on Paul in *Theology of the New Testament,* vol. 1. The material emphasizes that a person cannot have a right relationship to his environment—that is, control of his physical surroundings—unless he has a right relationship to himself and to the people about him. A discussion designed to elicit two points follows the presentation:

1. The problem of poverty can best be attacked by a person-centered work which helps people to gain control of themselves so that they can then control their environment. Translated into program, this usually means an attack upon poverty beginning with an emphasis upon community organization and personal relationships, as opposed to bulldozers and whitewash.

2. This kind of work requires some systematic understanding of the nature of man and the dimensions of his personality.

The presentation discussion helps the worker see that the problem may not be "shiftless, oversexed, alcoholic, no-good niggers" but rather immature, misshapen human beings whose intellectual, emotional, physical, and spiritual dimensions have not been developed adequately.

Such a background provides a guideline for program development. If the poor person has been denied in given areas of his personality, then, after gaining his confidence and trust, the worker must seek to involve him in a program designed to compensate for his particular inadequacies.

OVERVIEW

Interpersonal and intergroup conflicts fester where people do not have ongoing contact with one another. Without the reality factor of direct feedback, misperceptions continue to complicate individual living and to threaten society's cohesion. Every task must take account of the persons involved, and persons must be engaged in meaningful tasks. The small-group process provides a method that can combine personal relationships with structural power. When the group process is part of an organization or system, it provides a base for personal contact in the midst of stressful experience. In addition, it serves as a forum for an educational interpretation of the needs and aspirations of the "outs" and of the fears and resistances of the "ins."

The application of small-group process is varied, depending upon the setting. We have considered its use in community organization, public schools, and civil rights activity. It is most effective when people of diverse backgrounds who have ongoing contact with each other are able to be honest about their deeper fears and hopes. Then the mysterious enigma of people recedes, and they are able to know where they are in realistic ways. When people see relationships and group behaviors more clearly, constructive changes take place.

Ten

...I Am a White Racist

I am a white racist.

Until the first week in March, 1969, I did not know that I was a racist. I thought that I could and did control whatever prejudice I had. In fact, unless I really backed away from my involvements and examined myself with "theoretical" insight, I could discern no racist virus in me.

I was a good man—understanding, firm, broad-gauged, accepting. I was not like those other white people—biased, prejudiced, blind, vindictive, condescending. I gave time and energy to causes of human dignity. I stood up for those who were condemned by others. I respected blacks because I could and would "confront" them—for their sakes as well as mine. In short, like the drinker who does not see that he *is* an alcoholic, I was a racist who did not know it.

Let me tell my story, the circumstances that at last have forced me to see my racist sickness.

HITTING BOTTOM

On Sunday, March 2, 1969, at 1:30 P.M. the nineteen black students at Colgate Rochester Divinity School/Bexley Hall staged a take-over and a lockout. For eighteen days a black flag flew from the tower. For eighteen days these students remained locked in the building complex that included every major aspect of the institution except dormitories. For eighteen days no one entered the building except to convey information or to discuss strategy. For eighteen days students, faculty, and administration worked feverishly, in many cases around the clock, to find a resolution to the barricade and its implications.

What were the issues? Even to ask the question in terms of issues—plural—suggests the racist pattern, but let me hold that for a moment. On December 12, 1968, the black students had presented the school (not just the administration, but the school —faculty, students, and trustees) with a list of "demands." Note that their own rhetoric is easily misunderstood by whites, as, for example, "demands" are the equivalent of "issues." They wanted to name one-third of the board of trustees, the four pending faculty appointments, and administrative staff persons in recruitment-placement and in the church field education program. They gave the school until March 1 to meet their demands.

The following summary suggests something of what transpired between December 12 and March 1. For the first time in the history of the school two black women were hired to work in the offices as secretaries. The committee on faculty appointments, which included one black and one white student as voting members, agreed to consider only black candidates. The first and only black professor had been hired during the previous year, although attempts had been made in the past to hire a black professor. The nominating committee of the board of trustees, upon vote of the executive committee, was proceeding to nominate seven blacks out of a slate of eleven at the annual meeting in May. The first and only black trustee had been elected in 1967.

On Friday, February 28, at an all-school meeting, those facts were presented by the president. Almost everyone—white—agreed that the school was showing good faith and moving ahead on the demands of the Black Caucus. While there was some apprehension over the March 1 deadline, there was general optimism that this was enough to discourage and prevent anything unfortunate from happening.

Throughout the first four days of the barricade the demands appeared to escalate. Faculty and trustees, despite their initial disappointment over the action of the blacks, tried to be reasonable and to negotiate. The Black Caucus stood hard and firm. Even though there were internal disagreements among the blacks, they continued to hold their position.

Although bigots react to racial confrontation with open contempt and hatred, white liberals tend to react, according to Kenneth Clark and as borne out by my experience, with hurt combined with expressions of continuing and forgiving friendship. We kept referring to the blacks as colleagues. Such forbearing only intensified the frustrated rage and guilt of the black, adding to his already overburdened sense of self.

> When a Negro responds with anger to an act or attitude that seems to him discriminatory, he is often regarded as having violated the rules of conduct among gentlemen. He has not been amiable. He would seem, therefore, to have no way out. The choice is to alienate his friends or to suffer a sense of self-alienation.[1]

Any good psychologist knows (and I consider myself to be a good psychologist) that people learn who they are by bumping up against kind yet firm limits. So, by the fourth day, I, along with many other whites, was at the point of drawing a hard line: thus far, and no farther. We considered that the blacks were being unreasonable, rigid, and inflexible. Their grandiosity had gotten the better of them. As one white student put it, "You guys have won the ball game but you haven't looked at the scoreboard and don't know it."

It was during the evening of the fourth day and the morning of the fifth day that I realized I was a white racist. The evidence is so startlingly obvious. Why had I not seen it before?

Blacks had been telling whites for years—decades—a century at least. I had read Baldwin, Fanon, Malcolm X, King, and Carmichael. My black friends had been telling me for years. The black students had been telling us for nearly a decade.

But we—I—had not heard. I had not seen. I did not understand. Even with the take-over lockout, I, an expert in communication skills still was not hearing.

THE ISSUE

The *issue,* the *demand* (singular, not plural) is shockingly simple. The facts of the matter must not be allowed to obscure the truth of the matter. The point is this: who is first and who is second; who initiates and who responds; who asks and who answers; who drives and who rides?

For 350 years Negroes have had to wait to respond *until they were told* that they were needed. For fifteen years, Negroes have served as consultants, advisers, auxiliary resources, and invited experts. For years Negroes have been made to feel *and* to know that "the rate of change in their status [was] to be determined by the willingness of whites to accept them as human beings." [2] Despite sit-ins, walkouts, riots, and lockouts, blacks were still seen as consultants to the white power structures.

I, as a white faculty member, was to have the final say as to whether a potential colleague, including a black colleague, was acceptable. Regardless of every psychological analysis, regardless of every educational consideration, regardless of my good white intentions, in the end "the situation" remained the same.

Numbers are a symbol of the issue and because a symbol participates in that which it symbolizes, numbers are important. But numbers of trustees, faculty, administration, and staff were issue*s,* not *the* issue. The issue—the demand, as finally I am beginning to learn from my black brothers and sisters—is the reversal of role responsibility. Am I as a white willing to entrust circumstances that affect not only black people, but me also, to the judgment and responsibility of blacks? Am I as a white willing to put whatever fantasies I harbor of black violence, black indolence, black irresponsibility, black vindictiveness, and black incompetence on the line of reality to be tested? Am I as a white willing to face facts instead of living with illusions?

Concretely, that implies that in any decision affecting blacks particularly, the power of responsibility must reside with a black majority. Blacks thereby carry major responsibility; whites minor responsibility. Blacks invite whites as consultants and advisers as they (blacks) see the need and the necessity for such opinions. Blacks are now "insisting on being their own spokesmen; they are asking the whites to join them, either as equals or even in subordinate roles." [3] Not only is the judgment of blacks as adequate and as limited as that of whites, but even more in the historical period of the last third of the twentieth century the judgment of blacks must take priority over that of whites. Blacks know better than whites the dynamics of the present. Blacks know better than whites the nature of the road we are driving. Blacks are less likely to make wrong historical choices than whites, no matter how well-intentioned, well-informed, and appropriate may be the choices of whites, and more likely to make appropriate historical choices.

But even as I spell out the implications of my white racism in the area of responsibility, my selective blindness rears its ugly head. The issue of prudent judgment—that is, appropriate historical choices—is secondary. The issue of *trust* is primary, for the presence of distrust is deep. I must be willing to trust my life to blacks—regardless—unconditionally.

Of course (to say "of course" also reflects my racist residue by virtue of feeling the necessity of making the obvious point), I would expect to share responsibility in those activities affecting me. While I no longer expect to carry a major role, I do intend to carry a supportive, shared, and collaborative role. Frankly, I do not know how I would feel about my school becoming a "black" institution, by which I mean that a majority of trustees, administration, faculty, staff, and students would be black. I think if I wanted to work in a "black" institution, I ought to follow a former dean of Harvard University and join the faculty of a primarily Negro institution. I think there is a difference between a "black school" and a "black presence" in a school. But as yet I am still unclear.

RACIST DYNAMICS

If you have any acquaintance with alcoholism, by now you must be aware that I am illustrating my idea of racist confession with the model of the alcoholic.[4] This is no arbitrary comparison. Racism and alcoholism reveal similar dynamics:

1. Both interfere frequently or continuously with important life adjustments and interpersonal relationships.
2. Both must be acknowledged to be interfering before the patterns can be interrupted.
3. Both are permanent disturbances for which no cure is possible, but for which real relief is available.
4. Both continue to wreak havoc until the individual (or institution) "hits bottom."
5. Both create a circle of tragedy that affects and is affected by everyone involved.
6. Both hold out hope for renewal of life's possibilities *after* the bottom has been reached.

Let me touch briefly upon each of these points.

Interference with satisfying and effective living.

The disruption within my own institution, as well as the disruption in society at large, gives painful testimony to the consequences of white racism. The Kerner Commission Report on Civil Disorder warned in 1968 that as a society we were moving rapidly into two separate, suspicious, and hostile societies—one black, the other white. The follow-up report one year later informed us that we were even more dangerously close to such hostile camps than we had been. But even the report reflects unconscious racism, for it "presupposes that at one time there was one society" when in fact there never has been such a thing as "one society." [5]

If institutionally and organizationally effective sharing is doubtful, socially and personally satisfying relationships are virtually impossible. One's liking or not liking a person of another race has dissolved into an empty and insulting issue for blacks. Rights, not relationships, are what count. Dignity, not friendship, is the concern. Close contact always carries the burden of excessive sensitivity by whites and excessive suspiciousness by blacks. What "feels" like real friendship is viewed by blacks as ending in white betrayal and black bitterness and is experienced by whites as dissolving into black confrontation and white guilt.

Release requires acknowledgement.

An alcoholic can never say "I am an alcoholic" until he has recognized, accepted, and acknowledged his problem drinking. Only after he has stopped is he able to own *his* alcoholism. Only after he admits his inability to stop is he able to stop. Only after he sees the consequences of his behavior is he able to give up his self-destructive behavior.

Similarly, a white racist (I am referring only to white racists—blacks, browns, reds, and yellows will have to speak for themselves) can never say "I am a racist" until he has recognized, accepted, and acknowledged his racist blindness. Only after he stops selective inattention is he able to *own* his racism. Only after he sees the consequences of his orientation is he able to give up his self-destructive orientation.

No permanent cure but temporary relief.

Like an alcoholic, a racist must recognize that he can never be cured. The disease waits to break out and take over at every moment. The first response sets off the whole chain of racist reactions.

Consequently, I must accept the ever-present fact of my disease. Rather than deluding myself into believing that I can be cured or that I am cured, I must take one day at a time. I have no control over tomorrow. I may slip, and I *will* slip. But perhaps, just perhaps, I can make it through the next twenty-four hours without slipping.

The consequences.

Like drinking problems, racist problems begin early. There is an unconscious identification with "superior" white values. As black demands escalate, the racist falls back on his ingrained racist patterns. He claims that the blacks are excessive, unreasonable, wanting too much too soon, and unappreciative of the advances that have been made. The disruptive threat tends to be confined to one area of the institution, such as a course on black culture, but the institutional stability is maintained.

Then personal and social relationships are struck. The blacks enter into a vigorous resegregation pattern that may be abusive at worst or abrasive at best. There comes increasing isolation with its accompanying uncomfortableness and decreasing trust with its accompanying suspiciousness.

Each time the white fails to see his racist pattern the conflict deepens. Eventually, the racist reaches bottom when he confronts the bankruptcy of everything he has counted on and valued. Such is a typical racist pattern of deterioration.

Everyone involved is affected by and affects the circle of tragedy.

Like an alcoholic, a racist cannot expect those whom he harms not to feel and not to express hostility toward him for his sickness. Like an alcoholic, neither need a racist assume *all* the responsibility for the heartache and hardship of those involved. All virtue does not reside in the oppressed nor does all vice rest in the oppressor.

Al-Anon exists for the spouse of the alcoholic and Al-A-Teens for the children of the alcoholic. In these groups the "harmed" confess and explore *their* responsibility for what has taken place.

If I, a racist, have acted for the black in the past, he has allowed me so to act. My action is clearly my responsibility; his reaction is clearly his responsibility. It rests upon me to deal with myself; it rests upon him to deal with himself. And by barricading himself in the building, he was, indeed, taking responsibility.

Renewal of possibility after the bottom has been reached.

Like an alcoholic, the racist is without hope until the consequences of his orientation become greater than the advantages of avoiding it. Then, an upward cycle begins.

Alcoholics Anonymous can report many success stories. These are testimonies by men and women whose lives had been lost because of drinking and for whom life had been recovered because of Alcoholics Anonymous. As yet, I know of no comparable group that could be known as "Racists Anonymous." Testimonies of racist recovery are not readily at hand. As a society we seem not to have hit bottom.

The institution at which I teach appears to have come as close to the bottom as any I know by virtue of its total structural response that has been spelled out above. Whether or not we have learned, only time will tell. If we haven't, more severe tragedy lies ahead. If we have, we can only go up. Lost dignity will be restored. Lost resources will be recovered. Lost hope will be renewed. Lost life will be resurrected.

I have only realized my white racism for a short while. I am still dizzy from the discovery. I have much to learn. I must bump up against everything in my life once again. But I trust I am not the same self-righteous pharisee that I was.

At this point, for me to be a racist does not entail my giving up my identity, my needs, my insights, my ideas, or my position. I still argue. I still push. I still disagree. I still agree. I still am pushed. I still have to be convinced. In that respect I still am "me." And that "me-ness" is of crucial importance in keeping me free from my racist disease.

One expression of racial freedom lies in the ability of whites to argue with blacks as easily and as openly as with whites. White guilt and black fear are not transcended by tiptoeing around differences and conflict. The disease of racism cannot be arrested by refusing to touch the tender spots in one's relationships and work. The perpetuation of good intentions cannot be interrupted without significant changes in the structures of power. So, I still am my own person with my own peculiar mixture of abrasive goodwill. *But* my contribution now comes within a reordered context of power and participation.

Chaos, confusion, conflict, furor, ferment, friction, and fear —yes. Without these inevitable experiences there can be no reality in black-white contact. With them there may be renewed possibility of a truer humanity. The Christian message claims that people can be freed from past guilt and past fear *in order to live* toward the future:

    if we can confess our failure before God and another,

    if justice is sought through reordered and shared effort,

    if we do allow hurt to be healed.

I know the "old Adam" is still with me. Like an alcoholic, once a racist always a racist. But like an alcoholic, a confessed one has a chance of a renewed life. Only time, tragedy, and teaching by blacks will help me to sharpen and sustain this refocusing of my world.

I am groping for what Robert Terry has called the new white consciousness. Rather than being color blind, whites must be color conscious; that is seeing how color consciousness is used by one people against another people. What is demanded of whites is that we understand ourselves "simultaneously as white racists and as creators of justice." [6] *"What is at stake for white America today is not what black people want and do but what white people stand for and do."* [7]

What is expected of whites (of me) is not that we (I) confess our (my) racism but that we (I) change our (my) ways!

Eleven

Black Barricade and Beyond: Structural Change

For white America to understand
the life of the black man,
it must recognize that
so much time has passed and so little has changed.[1]

The specter of black students carrying guns emerging from the barricaded building at Cornell, in the spring of 1969, remains stamped upon the memory of white America. Lockouts, take-overs, and confrontations have become the daily diet of educational institutions. Industry, business, and government recoil from the impact of their own manifestations of the barricade phenomenon.

Those whom society has passively ignored and actively rejected refuse to remain invisible nonentities any longer. The last are becoming first. The first are learning they are to be last.

Every part of society lurches with nonnegotiable demands. Whites wonder what is happening. Blacks know what they have been denied. Although to whites the eruptions and demands seem unintelligible, they are neither random nor chaotic. But what is the order? What is the meaning?

This discussion deals only with racial aspects of our current cultural disruption and not with the wider issues raised in student protests, but the patterns of group interactions are similar.

To draw my parallel, in speaking for the class of 1970 at

Bowdoin College, George S. Isaacson pointed out that "the mood of discontented youth has shifted 'from frustration to anger and from anger to action.' " [2] In assaulting what they consider to be the injustices of America, students, he said, are calling for

> "a new alliance of the angry. . . . Discontent should not be the property of just the young, the black and the radical. We should not be confused by considering ourselves separated by generations. We are a nation of people, not students, and as a people we must act together." [3]

Let me analyze racial developments at my own institution. I have already touched on the core of the matter in the previous chapter. Now I want to examine the dynamics of the changes. By this analysis I hope to suggest the applicability of those developments to larger social issues, for the Divinity School may be regarded as a society in miniature. What happened to the Divinity School gives clues to what has happened, and is happening, and can happen elsewhere.

As an educational institution, Colgate Rochester Divinity School/Bexley Hall/Crozer has not been exempt from racial tension. The demand for change has been there as everywhere. The extent of structural change, however, is unique.

How is it that the Black Caucus of only nineteen members could trigger a reorganization of the institution? For that, in fact, is what took place. In a white institution, one-third of the members of the board of trustees are black by vote at the annual meeting in May, 1969. Four key faculty appointments are black as a result of a faculty decision making that top priority. Staff and administrative personnel (in the offices of dean of students, director of field education, and dean of admissions) include black personnel. And, even more importantly, these changes have come as black students assumed primary responsibility—initiative and effective power—in decision-making processes, while faculty, administration, and trustees assumed secondary responsibility—review and legal power—at these points.

Parallel to developments in the country at large, yet distinctive by virtue of its being a small (180-190) graduate, theological, educational institution with a history of trying to cope with black/white conflict, the racial crisis at the school shows an historical development. Its unfolding tends to be orderly, progressive, and in touch with what has taken place in other educational institutions.

PHASES OF CHANGE

A description of events over the last decade suggests a logical development. The following phases are agreed upon by those who participated. Some of the particulars found their clearest expression in the small-group process referred to in chapter 9. There the confrontations and encounters gave the most sensitive readings as to where we were institutionally.

Blind Integration, 1958-1961

Prior to 1961, the Negro students did not constitute a large enough group for them to feel the significance of their presence at the School. Nor did the School feel their presence. Even though blacks talked informally of the Freedom Movement, they kept their "peace." While that represented a somewhat unhealthy accommodation to the School, likewise it reflected the apathetic helplessness and hopelessness of so many blacks as voiced by Eldridge Cleaver during the same period:

> I'd always known that I was black, but I'd never really stopped to take stock of what I was involved in. I met life as an individual and took my chances. . . . we lived in an atmosphere of novocain. Negroes found it necessary, in order to maintain whatever sanity they could, to remain somewhat aloof and detached from "the problem." [4]

Gradually, the "atmosphere of novocain" wore off. Racial pain began to be experienced within the School. Whites only dimly sensed the widespread experience of many Negroes of feeling second-rate, second-place, second-class.

Whites had no awareness of the historical link between Negro mentality and the absolute dependency and deeply conscious personal inferiority of the slave. What the authors of *Black Rage* call "the postal-clerk syndrome" in which the ideal black is portrayed as "passive, nonassertive, and nonaggressive," making a virtue of identification with the aggressor and adopting "an ingratiating and compliant manner," [5] was completely incomprehensible.

The distortion of the post-Reconstruction "magnolia myth" of Negroes happy with docility was equally incomprehensible to both blacks and whites. For it completely obliterated awareness of the black fight for freedom in which, for instance, between 1663 and 1884, there were a hundred recorded Negro revolts in this country and no fewer than fifty-five recorded Negro revolts on the high seas. [6]

For Negroes during that time the symbolic meaning of their predominantly acquiescing behavior can be understood as a passive congeniality, on the one hand, with an ambivalence of lonely anxiousness on the other. To this, whites responded with support, encouragement, and help. In many respects, it can be viewed as a continuation of the slave-master symbiotic relationship in which each needed the other in order to maintain personal security.

Generally, the Negro experienced himself without power and therefore with questionable worth, while perceiving the white as endowed with both power and worth.

Cooperative Civil-Rights Activism, 1961-1964

By 1961, Negro students began to describe the raw sores of Rochester's inner city. They reported about police brutality, discriminatory housing, and the tubercular abscesses of gracious Southern culture in Northern guise. The Negro preacher was viewed as "a hustler," polarizing the black population into the overly good and the exaggeratedly bad, while anesthetizing blacks to whiteys' injustices. Although the Black Muslims were just hitting the national media, Negro students were thoroughly cognizant of them. White oppression and Negro acquiescence hammered on their souls.

Two mutually exclusive tendencies appeared. The most angry and alienated of the more secular blacks withdrew from active involvement in the School. They attended classes yet met only the minimum of expectations. In the small groups they sat shut off in isolated indifference.

The more cooperative blacks kept mobilizing support for civil rights causes. They talked of what was happening "out there." They shared their turmoil in school when "brothers and sisters" were "putting their bodies on the line."

Both groups tended to be lower-middle class, primarily from the Midwest. They feared *and* experienced that their education was cutting them off from the brotherhood.

By means of personal sharing and social interpretations, the cooperating Negroes evoked white responses. Simultaneously, they were held suspect by their more bitter brothers. Experiences in Selma, Birmingham, and Washington moved from reports by participating black and white students and faculty to more community-wide recitals of the exodus from bondage to freedom.

In some instances, whites felt pressured into acting yet withheld their reservations because of their own uneasy guilt or their fear of personal reprisals by those involved.

The period from 1961 to 1964 presented a spread of interaction. It ranged from rebellious disappointment to leadership encouragement and direction for white involvement. Whites adapted to black concerns with fairly wholehearted cooperation. In the spring of 1964, fourteen black and white students were arrested for chaining themselves across a major thoroughfare at rush hour to protest a landlord's refusal to rent an apartment to a Negro social worker.

In 1964, black seminarians witnessed the Rochester Riot and the passage of the Civil Rights Act. Instead of easing pressure, the legislation aggravated it by reminding blacks of their continued rejection and second-class status. The "surprise" of white Rochesterians at the explosion in the ghetto fanned bitter cynicism. The objective issues of overcrowded and restricted housing, of marginal and menial employment, or of questionable and irrelevant education receded. In their wake poured what Kenneth Clark refers to as "the subjective dimensions" of "resentment, hostility, despair, apathy, self-depreciation, and its ironic companion, compensatory grandiose behavior." [7]

By 1963, blacks comprised about 7 percent of the student body. That proportion, combined with stresses in the country, could be said to mark the transition from Negro tokenism to black presence. The storm below the surface of compliance and cooperation broke out in full fury.

Resegregation with Abusiveness, 1963-1967

Increasingly, Negro students matriculated from the South. While the "integrated" atmosphere of the School tended to make them dizzy with undreamed-of possibilities, especially for contact with white women, within weeks a deep revulsion would set in. They jumped from affiliative to angry responses. Whereas, previously, the angrier blacks had passively withdrawn, now most blacks actively cut themselves off. They abused staff and students alike, suggesting that this phase be described as resegregation with abusiveness.

The School found itself embroiled in resegregation with a vengeance. The small groups served as the one place blacks and whites could not avoid each other. Blacks made it plain that they had no intention of being pleasant to whites. Any exchange was phony and demeaning. Communication with whitey was impossible!

Despite such declarations of the futility of communication, black students continually bombarded the groups with discourses on black nationalism, black culture, and black cynicism. Discussions vacillated between racial clash, in which blacks blistered whites and whites allowed themselves to be blistered, and racial content, in which blacks informed whites of black culture and whites were curious to learn about black dynamics. At every opportunity black students interpreted racial oppression with aggression and anger.

Quietly at first, then with growing conviction, black religion took on significance. For the students, the black church constitutes their key hope. Only in the church, they believe, can blacks

> be free of white domination,
> express emotion,
> exercise leadership, and
> experience genuine identity.

Only in black worship and black preaching can integrity be combined with justice.

With the rediscovery of their heritage and identity, "blackness" changed from a negative to a positive value. Understandably, therefore, the segregated church will be the last institution to desegregate. It remains the one clear, sure sphere in which blacks *know* the freeing of the free ones. On this point blacks can be called racist with justification. Probably there will be no movement in the near future to desegregate the black church. Indeed, the autonomous nature of the black church stands as a catalyst for political, educational, and economic reform. It can continue so, apparently, only by remaining black.

By the mid-sixties, resegregation had shifted the dynamics of group interaction. Blacks moved from more submissive agreeableness toward an increasingly tyrannous antagonism. In the abusive period, fighting, even brutality, predominated. Beneath these surface behaviors could be sensed feelings of impotent bitterness and cynical resistance. In reaction, whites exhibited passive resistance, distrust and inferiority, apathy and hurt. They were frankly bewildered and baffled, a typical reaction in such confrontation.

Even though whites were still perceived as powerful super-devils, they ceased to be objects of esteem. If blacks could not respect themselves, nevertheless they abandoned respect for whites. If whites no longer openly patronized blacks, nevertheless they experienced confusion about their own worth.

The abusive pattern can be understood as part of what William Grier and Price Cobbs have termed the static "underpinnings of the new black militancy." Many who "preach blackness seem headed blindly toward self-destruction, uncritical of anything 'black' and damning the white man for diabolical wickedness." [8] Those blacks have seized upon the earlier development of Malcolm X, ignoring the fact that he had outgrown such exaggeration by the time of his assassination.

Whites want to know whether they must settle for black sadism and white masochism. Blacks long to move beyond white guilt and black anger. But what can break the deadlock? Clearly and obviously, *only the painful therapy of real change!* Such a transition tenderly showed itself in 1965, gaining momentum as the School moved into 1967 and 1968.

Resegregation with Abrasiveness, 1966-1968

From cries of generalized racism, black students began to zero in on specific instances of racism. These ranged from inadequate curriculum for ministry in the black church, to discrimination in the refectory, to lack of faculty and administration involvement in urban conflict. Instead of being simply abusive, blacks became progressively abrasive about particulars.

White students underwent a similar modification. From having been "fed up" with the racial clash, they began to sense their own cultural deprivation and sickness. No longer did they accept the attitude that blacks were deprived and sick while whites were rich and healthy. They started to see the pervasive nature of racial antagonism.

White racism and corporate guilt began to make sense. As Malcolm X once explained in interpreting the meaning of "white devils": "Unless we call one white man, by name, a 'devil,' we are not speaking of any *individual* white man. We are speaking of the *collective* white man's *historical* record." He went on to point out, however, that if any individual white man might be free of corporate guilt, no individual black man is free of corporate consequences. "You cannot find *one* black man, I do not care who he is," he contended, "who has not been personally damaged in some way by the devilish acts of the collective white man!" [9]

While tension continued in the small groups, abuse receded. In one group, in the spring of 1966, a black told how good it felt to stand in the dormitory hall and shout, "All white people are dumb," along with other colorful broadsides. A former white "friend" questioned the value of simply letting out anger that way. He was informed that if he had stepped out in the hall and shouted, "All niggers are dumb," he would have gotten an immediate response!

When the white protested he did not feel that way, the black insisted, "That really isn't the issue. What matters is not ignoring us. You need to stand up and fight back instead of just standing there taking whatever is handed out to you." He was asking for a valid and vigorous "over againstness" on the part of whites.

As whites continued to complain of the "never ending" racial clash/discussion, blacks snapped back, "But we have to live with it all the time."

One second-year group, during the spring of 1967, provided the arena for the unfolding developments. The group consisted of two whites, who eventually ran for student-body officers, two women students, one of the most militant blacks, a very sympathetic white identifier with the blacks, and several other whites. The black member occasionally came conspicuously late, often ignored the group by writing in a notebook, and sometimes put his head on the table and closed his eyes.

One day the group picked up a comment by the black student that he often anticipated, expected, and, as two members suggested, perhaps even wanted rejection from whites. He went on to explain that he had not suffered as much as many blacks. He had advantages they did not have. Thus, he passionately longed to identify with them. When he was not rejected, his equilibrium was upset.

The two who had raised the issue went on to discuss other kinds of role conflict. In contrast to the cultural differences described, one woman linked discrimination against blacks with discrimination against women. Both were obviously "visible." No woman could escape being a woman; no black could escape being a black.

That day the group experienced some unfreezing of its stereotypes. Those who had been tangling with the black seemed able to generalize from his experience to their experiences. He, in turn, allowed the possibility that some of the ways he came on hard grew out of his need to compensate for lacks he felt.

Late that spring, student elections were held. On the preceding evening, blacks accused the two white nominees of being racists. Unless they withdrew, the blacks promised to beat them up. The whites refused. No such physical attack ever came, but that night the dormitory was patrolled. The next day at an all-school luncheon, the blacks publicly demanded that the nominees withdraw. Though deeply shaken, the two stood firm.

At the next session of the group, the now-elected president asked the militant black where he was in relation to all that had gone on.

In a relatively calm voice the black described how the hostility was as deeply felt then as in the outbreak. For the first time, he felt, the brothers were welded together. At last, he declared, the school was being forced to face the implications of its racist attitudes.

In assessing the semester's experience in the group, the white sympathizer stated, "It was like *No Exit:* hell was being with each other. In the group we had to relate." The black also thought the group structure "very good." For him it sharpened the polarization in the school, making him experience it and enabling him to accept it more fully. Now he could allow the distance between himself and the white world. Both the nominees felt the structure had forced them to deal with the black student in ways they would not otherwise have done. Such a process had been a learning experience. Despite the shouting, the confusion, the bewilderment, and the hostility, there was no way for the students to withdraw from the group. They had to confront each other each week. The structure had kept them dealing with the issues.

During that same semester of 1967, a black student in another group voiced deep anger and hurt that no white faculty member or student had attended a lecture on black history. To him our absence symbolized our indifference. If we really cared about him as a person, we would have tried to understand his history. Such hurt signaled the shift from abusive to abrasive styles.

Previously blacks had claimed whites could never understand. Now they began saying if whites would be more aggressive, *perhaps* they could understand.

Like whites, blacks want respect. Before 1967, almost all black seminarians felt ashamed of their culture and, especially, their church life. They needed to affirm their heritage and to experience whites acknowledging its worth. By this time, instead of rejecting the black church and black ministry as irrelevant or as merely an instrument for social change, many students began to affirm the intrinsic value of the black church as a community of faith. Black worship rapidly gained prominence in chapel.

In this abrasive phase, the blacks actively asserted competitive superiority while they modified passive-aggressive complaints about being victims of injustice. Whites, in turn, grew less antagonistic, more actively competitive, yet continued to act with uncertainty and ambivalence.

As long as the blacks remained overwhelmed and diffused, their interpersonal responses tended to be passive. They were forced to "devise individual ways to meet group problems." [10] When angry, they showed apathy and bitterness. When friendly, they appeared acquiescent and conforming. Because of the intensity of these patterns, both were maladaptive.

However, as isolated individuals coalesced into the Black Caucus, individual affiliative responses to the white culture decreased and hostile group responses increased. With that movement from frustration to anger to action, blacks felt less impotent and more powerful. With increasing strength came the beginnings of dignity; with dignity came feelings of worth; with worth vitality took root.

Aware that they were a group, the blacks shifted their energies from generalized antagonism to focused militancy. From then on they acted and reacted as The Black Caucus. What Kenneth Clark has called "the rules of the ghetto" took over. They presented "to the hostile white world a single voice of protest and rebellion," even as they would allow no issue to "take precedence over the basic issue of race and, specifically, of racial oppression." [11]

By now white confusion undermined former feelings of white power and white worth. Some began to regret their whiteness and wished they could be black. Others, out of desperation, took up the group strategy, forming The White Caucus.

Although the caucuses functioned as separate and autonomous groups, they did team up to press common causes, such as the installation of a black professor who could articulate the concerns of blackness. With hopes rising, aggressive agitation mounted. As in the larger society, personal and group action reinforced each other. The vicious cycle of personal and community powerlessness had been interrupted. "A truly hopeless group makes no demands and certainly does not insist upon stark social confrontations." [12] At last, blacks were harnessing their repressed and diffused rage into anger energy for the purpose of effecting structural change.

Tentative Political Collaboration, 1967-1968

Blacks were now organized to structure presence into the institution. Whites also pushed black presence for themselves as well as for the blacks. They argued that nobody could be prepared for ministry today without grappling with blackness.

The assassination of Martin Luther King, Jr., transformed an anticipated confrontation between the school and the Black Caucus into a memorial celebration that launched an $800,000 campaign, conducted by the caucus, to endow a professorship in black church studies and to establish memorial scholarships.

The blacks exercised militant leadership. Whites, in turn, consented and cooperated. Blacks now experienced not only power but worth, not only prominence but appreciation. They were demonstrating the black solidarity which Malcolm X saw as necessary before there could be black-white solidarity.[13] Whites felt less abused by black aggression. They understood it more.

A taped excerpt from the final session of an advanced seminar in pastoral care and counseling reflects the mood of spring, 1968. A black student shares his excitement:

> I feel rather joyful. I feel a sense of triumph, too, because during my three years here it was hell for me. I see some things happening now I never thought would happen. I'm glad, too, that I was in a sense a part of the thing that brought this thing into being. At the time, it [the antagonism] was a bit irrational and very extreme on our part, but I see some growth beyond that stage. In a sense I do not make any apology for it because some real fruits have come from this.
>
> In a sense I feel that a new day has taken place for me and with the school. And yet we are living in some very critical times. I cannot say when I leave this school whether I will be in a comfortable and secure

place or not. I might be burned in the burning, too. I don't know. But I still can feel at this moment a sense of hope. I can say that as one of the black students that, in a sense, (I take some pride in saying this): we have a *good* thing going here; we have a real thing going! It was tragic that King's death came; I'm sorry that that happened. But out of this, something happened.

But even before that something else was happening. It was happening all along. And now it has finally come into something real.

In this group I have confronted some people and they have confronted me. I think that the confrontation has produced some change.

The white nominee for student body president the previous year responds:

That's something I want to finish up. I don't want to interrupt you, but I want to say that I still feel fairly distant from you and from all the black students. But I think even that is progress. I was so out of it I did not even know that I did not understand before, that I did not have a clue of what it was like, of what kind of a world we are living in.

And you helped—you personally, and you the black community. This process here in the last three years saved me from being one of those guys that said, "Good enough for King. He got what he deserved." You really saved me. I have a long ways to go but maybe, maybe, you got me started. You sure turned me around. I needed that. I could not have done it. I could not even know that I was distant. Thank you.

The black student goes on:

Yeh, I just think back to those times. That was during the time when I felt, "Boy, with these kind of people here, nothing ever, ever will take place." And now, we sit here with you, even though we are distant. You and I participate in a new day. I didn't think, you didn't even think, that this would take place.

The white nominee agrees:

I didn't think it would take place. I didn't even know it *needed* to take place; I was so far out. I feel I am just getting to the point where I cannot much more than realize that something needs to be done. Before, I didn't even realize that.

A white activist picks up another facet of the dynamics:

At first I had been pretty involved in the whole White Caucus thing. Then, to see the process move into a stage where I was not needed any longer (because of the Black Caucus). In a way it has been very, very hard for me to let you guys (blacks) *be,* to let you do your own thing and to do it without my even knowing about it, and not wanting to snoop around and find out what you're doing. It's like I had been

sort of paternalistic, you know. I do regard black people still, in the
deepest part of my being, as somehow still children or something. It's
so hard to let you be and not want to take credit for your lives. I
think I can do it much better now than I used to. Up until this semester
I did not really know how I am indebted to you guys. And I am, and
I thank you.

A white, concerned about black "oversensitivity" to race,
continues:

It sounds like a bandwagon, but I'll always remember your saying "the
church has sold out to the culture." You told me that for a solid year,
and I got so I would put it in the margins (of my notes). Five times
you got that into the Old Testament class. What's that got to do with
Old Testament? (That was my attitude.) Now I can smile about it
because I think this was part of that year you were hating us and
hating the institution.

You were one of the first blacks I really encountered. The day I
could say to you, "Hey, Black Boy!" and you could say to me, "What
do you want, Whitey?" meant something. I was not scared any more.

The black student concludes wistfully:

The first year we were here we had it. We had it! I remember that in
one of the small groups a white student was sitting across the table
from me, and I jumped up and yelled, "I'll take no shit from you!" It
was a very hostile period. My mind goes back to that. Those were
some terrible days, dark days. I imagine it took the darkness to have
some light or to know the light. I sort of wish I was going to be around
next year.

In November, 1968, over eight hundred people crowded into
the main hall of the chamber of commerce to hear that the caucus
had raised $200,000 and that the school was committed to fol-
lowing through. As gospel singer Mahalia Jackson sang and
talked "soul power" in contrast to "black power," Dr. and Mrs.
Martin Luther King, Sr., shared themselves, and Dr. Ralph Aber-
nathy extolled Dr. King's vision of a new order transcending race,
creed, or nation, all felt that a new day had come.

My analysis of the change tends to distort the dynamics of the
negotiation and requires further interpretation. For instance, during 1968, the White Caucus demanded a black professor, not
because of a high affiliative tendency but because it saw its own
need for black presence. Thus, in this political collaborative phase,
black dominance was grounded in and submissive to black needs,
while white dominance was grounded in and submissive to white
needs! The collaborations arose only when both groups felt auton-

omy and responsibility. The difference, though, lay in the content of what those terms meant for the separate groups.

The whites had to realize that their autonomy was worthless if it did not respect the autonomy of the blacks. To show such respect, however, required not acquiescence in the negative sense of the term but a fresh comprehension of their needs, that is, of going beyond white ethnocentrism to a new white consciousness. With that new awareness they saw that simply to assert themselves in their old ways of behaving—cooperative civil rights, for example—was, in effect, to be dominant (i.e., white-centered) but not autonomous. In doing that they would fail to grapple with the hidden prejudices and hostilities that kept them cut off from their own autonomy. Thus, although they would have been behaving dominantly, they really would have been as submissive as the blacks.

Unfortunately, institutional lethargy and institutional racism continued to plague the school. The predicament was compounded by the process of assimilating Bexley Hall, an Episcopal school which moved to the campus during the summer. The period of political collaboration proved overly optimistic and naïve. Initially, the merger brought about some rough moments. In part that has been attributed to the fear by blacks that Bexley Hall brought with it the authority of established institutionalism.

Confrontation over Structural Issues, 1968-1969

After November's climax, the school found itself further besieged. An ultimatum by the Black Caucus at an all-school luncheon on December 12, 1968, giving a period until March 1, 1969, to meet its "nonnegotiable demands," plunged us at last into confrontation over central structural change. While the move lacked the political agility of other caucus moves, according to some observers, the demands came with dramatic power.

The climax came with the take-over described in the previous chapter. It was clearly an act precipitated by a minority of the Black Caucus. Even though it grew into concerted action, differences among the members divided the caucus. While concerned white students and faculty were "disappointed" in the use of such tactics, they nevertheless supported the purposes of the barricade.

At last the truth came home. The school had spoken much, acted little, and understood less. More unfortunately, actions had been taken *on behalf* of blacks, not *in concert with* blacks. The insensitivity of doing "for" instead of "with" black students exposed our institutional racism and our enlightened paternalism.

The nuances of group interaction in the collaborative phase assumed crucial importance in the confrontational period. During the lockout/lockin, many whites tended to be submissive and acquiescing, talking sentimentally about "love" and "colleagues" and "friends," when the issue was power, position, and structural change.

The White Caucus felt that it could not collaborate with integrity with the Black Caucus, even as the Black Caucus felt that the White Caucus had become impotent and a hindrance. The White Caucus was concerned with neither taking over nor calling in the police. What mattered to it was that whites come to an authentic understanding of their autonomy in relation to the total situation, especially to the blacks. In that way autonomy would avoid isolation and domination by asserting authentic whiteness. Such an assertion, they claimed, must always be open to negotiating over conflicting demands. Genuine identity has as part of its very nature the dynamic of contrast.

In this interaction between the groups, we can see black domination, direction, and dogmatic declarations as to what is to take place. The white reaction represents a greater docility, reluctant obedience, and grudging respect, but not without traces of weak submission and wary hurt. The warm mutuality of the tape excerpt has vanished.

The barricade produced too much hurt for any easy or euphoric personal relationships.

Something of the development of the black/white interaction can be sensed from the felt meaning of the kinds of "messages" sent by blacks during the various phases. In effect, I am simplifying dynamic and diverse experience, but the summary conveys the pattern.[14]

> Cooperative Civil Rights: "You are doing bad things to us."
> Abusive Resegregation: "Either you do this *or* that will happen."
> Abrasive Resegregation: "We don't give in until you come across with what we want."
> Tentative Collaboration: "We don't need you. Don't contact us. We'll contact you."
> Structural Confrontation: "This is the way things are or else," (with intimidating pressure as part of the tone of confident autonomy).

BEYOND THE BARRICADE

Now that the structural changes have come, the institution is moving into a more authentic pluralism. The presence of blacks in the board of trustees, administration, faculty, and staff allows for significant black presence *and* for obvious black diversity. Just as whites differ in purposes, values, motives, and methods; so do blacks. Our emerging pluralism takes color contrast as seriously as creedal contrast; yet it allows for collaborative actions based on peer relationships. Almost gone is the gracious thoughtfulness by those in power for those without power.

Since change, not relatedness, remains as the crucial issue, blacks *must* retain a managing, directing leadership pattern supported by competitive conflict and by collaborative responsibility. Because they started from a position of powerlessness, they have to find, establish, and assert their distinctive identity *before* they can risk moving too far toward adaptive identification with dominant cultural forms.

Whites, in turn, *must* appreciate this development by demonstrating trust in black leadership and by letting blacks set the terms of the interaction, even though there may be feelings of personal discomfort and apprehension.

It will be some time, and *only* as a consequence of accumulated changes, before the dominance-submissive interactions will be less exaggerated and more adaptive. Without the tension, pluralistic collaboration could easily regress into friendly agreeableness, dulling the necessity for institutional change.

Can blacks and whites live, learn, work, play, and worship together, or are their ways of life and kinds of need mutually exclusive?

Mounting evidence suggests separatism. An easy answer is unavailable.

Blacks at Colgate Rochester/Bexley Hall/Crozer question whether "black presence" can be significant. They doubt whether black church needs can be met in a white institution. Whites question whether such total disruption as the barricade with its "bombast" and such reorganization of trustees, administration, faculty, and students does not, in fact, undercut their needs.

The widespread support of the barricade, rooted in years of structured conflict and interpretation, suggests, despite deep reservations, that blacks and whites want to stem the avalanche of separatism. Difficult as conflicting needs and sharpened participation are, the task justifies the effort.

Tension and conflict are inevitable. Fears and frustrations are unavoidable. But . .

the alternative of not trying

is

indefensible *and* suicidal!

Twelve

Not As Strange As It Seems

In his play *Antony and Cleopatra,* Shakespeare describes the
frustrating experience of trying to understand something that
eludes understanding:

Lepidus: What manner o'thing is your crocodile?

Mark Antony: It is shaped, sir, like itself; and it is as broad
as it hath breadth; it is just so high as it is,
and moves with its own organs: it lives by that
which nourisheth it; and the elements once out
of it, it transmigrates.

Lepidus: What colour is it of?

Mark Antony: Of its own colour too.

Lepidus: 'Tis a strange serpent.[1]

Often our attempts to understand life prove just as frustrating.
When we ask what manner of thing life is, all we learn is that
life is like itself. Such tautology adds little to what we know.

Since man first started to think, he has tried to make sense
of his experience. Today, because of bombardment by so many
facts and the flood of so much information, the necessity to organize experience in some meaningful way is more compelling than
ever. Somehow we must find patterns into which to fit the fragments of information that are barraging us. Such conceptual frame-
works serve the dual functions of helping us to: (1) understand

185

more clearly and concretely the way in which life holds together, and (2) act upon that understanding for the purpose of fuller and more meaningful living.

A woman undergoing analytic therapy reported the following dream:

> I am making a ground plan, perhaps of a house and garden, in which several pieces have to be fitted into a given space. They will go in quite well, only first it is necessary to draw the circle showing the points of the compass, to give the orientation. I look for something with which to draw the circle.[2]

Without going deeply into the dynamics of the dream, it is immediately obvious that she was dealing with "the basic 'plan' of her [life and] personality." [3] How was she to arrange the parts— the different drives and trends—to fit into her life space appropriately and satisfactorily?

Deep within her is the confident trust that all "will go in quite well." The contrasts and opposites, in the end, constitute a living whole. Yet for that to come to pass she requires some kind of compass. Only by having an orientation and direction can she draw the circle to include everything.

As helping persons, we, too, need some kind of orientation, some kind of compass, some kind of frame of reference. Without it we are swept away by the rising tides of change or caught in hardening cement of constancy. The average adult can carry around in his head only about seven independent items of information at any one time. Such a limitation severely handicaps our handling that which comes at us. But by means of something analogous to a compass, we can orient ourselves more easily. We can organize what comes more systematically. We can then move through the world with more confidence and competence.

One aspect of exercising dominion and control over the created world, which is clearly the responsibility entrusted to us by God, is the construction of orienting compasses. We are not left in the position of saying that life is like life. That woman's dream (telling her that life made sense because it is orderly) is a concrete expression of the doctrine of Logos, the orderly structuring of existence. Obviously, there are many ways of conceiving of man and his world. Each of them has proven to be useful. None of them turns out to be ultimate. Even so, life need not be as strange as it seems.

For myself, I have come upon and am developing an orienting compass that I find fruitful both for understanding and for acting. This compass or analytic tool allows me to bring together in a single image structure ways in which we deal with the world and ways in which we relate to people.[4] Its dimensions and directions have emerged as I have lived with the kinds of experiences and reflections I have been sharing with you.

Of course, there is risk in such abstraction. In constructing a conceptual scheme the very act of generalization can falsify concrete experience. Nothing ever quite fits exactly. Even so, I am willing to take the risk. Whatever violence I commit because of this Procrustean bed is more than compensated for by my increasing ability to make sense of the world. Then, too, when the scheme does not fit, I simply put it aside and try something else. Thus I keep both humble and alert.

WORKING ASSUMPTIONS

Before describing the compass directly, it is necessary to set down five basic assumptions. These assumptions reduce the strangeness of life. They establish the nature of the compass. They influence the way it can be utilized.

Anxiety

The experience of anxiety governs everything we do. Anxiety may be conceived of as the gap between what is and what might be, the gap between the reality and the expectation, the gap between the known and the unknown.[5] More particularly, anxiety constitutes an attack upon or threat to our sense of self-esteem and self-worth.[6] In short, our very existence—biologically, psychologically, and spiritually—recoils at the prospect of destruction. Our security shakes at the foundations.

> When the gap opens up as a Grand Canyon, we pull back. The distance is too great. The danger is too much. We dare not risk destruction.

> When there is no gap, there is no tension, no possibility, no expectancy. All is connected, comfortable, secured. We have lost the necessary stress of life.[7]

> When the gap closes to a negotiable crevice, we move ahead. We are motivated to get across by some appropriate means.

The distance is manageable. The danger is stimulating. We dare to risk growth.[8]

What we do is activated by anxiety and is aimed at reducing that anxiety in order to enhance our existence.

Adaptive-Maladaptive

What we do may be appropriate or inappropriate, depending upon the circumstances of the moment. Situation ethics has only served to remind us that nothing we do is either absolutely, inherently, and inevitably bad or absolutely, inherently, and inevitably good. Everything has potentially adaptive and potentially maladaptive aspects.

The characteristic frequency and intensity of any bit of behavior suggests its appropriateness. We may come on too hard in a situation, thereby provoking a strong counterreaction in others. We may roll over and play dead at the very instant resistance is called for. In some form and in certain moments every kind of behavior is necessary for full human functioning.[9]

In ordinary experience the closest analogy to my point about the necessity for every kind of behavior might be the automatic washing machine. A load of wash is dumped in and evenly distributed around the center. Occasionally, during a cycle, some heavy pieces, such as towels or sheets, begin to overbalance the load. As the spinning increases, the load pulls more and more to one side, generating a violent off-balancing of the machine. When such a condition occurs, most washers automatically stop. By a redistribution of the load, balance is reestablished. The washing then continues.

Such is a picture of the balanced forces within the human personality. Every part is necessary for continuous and constructive functioning. When every part is fitted in and fitting properly, all goes well. When any part gets exaggerated or out of place, trouble follows.

A woman in her middle forties illustrates the point. She was facing the transition between her children's leaving home and her finding new ways of being a person. She reported the following dream:

> I was on top of a tall, thin tower. There was a woman at the bottom of the tower by the ladder that reached to the top. She wanted to climb up, and I told her not to. She did anyway.

When she got to the top, the tower collapsed. Instead of crashing to the ground, somehow the bricks came together and formed a new structure that was more of a rectangle, lower and broader. We landed safely on the new building without any harm.

Her investment of herself as a mother had grown constant and increasingly rigid over the years. She had neglected herself as an independent person with needs and desires of her own. Now the neglected side of her personality—the woman at the bottom of the ladder—was insisting upon being taken into account as much as the intended side of her personality—herself at the top of the tower.

The old form could not stand the strain of the new life force. It collapsed under the strain between the mother role from the past and the person-need in the present. But (and this is the point) all the elements of her personality were reassembled and used. The new building was lower and stabler than the old tower; yet in the midst of the change she knew the continuity of her self.

Behavior is adaptive or maladaptive depending upon when it comes and how intensely it is expressed.

Levels of Personality

Man is the only organism capable of being one way in his attitudes and seeming to be another way in his actions. Or, to put it more positively, we are complex creatures, complex by virtue of the levels of our personality.

> There is *"the level of overt public behavior."* Here we find the unintended yet actual behavior that can be observed and reported by others.
> There is *the personal level of conscious behavior.* Here we find the intended experience and behavior that we can report to others.
> There is *the desired level of fantasied experience and behavior.* Here we find the wishes and daydreams that express the underlying feelings of who we imagine ourselves to be.
> There is *the level of idealized experience and behavior.* Here we find the values and ideals, that we consciously cultivate, of the kind of person we think we ought to be.[10]

Each of these levels operates in a way that influences the person we are and the person we are becoming. To the degree these levels disclose similar patterns, we tend to be strong, stable, and consistent. To the degree the levels reflect conflicting or contrasting patterns, we tend to be uncertain, unpredictable, and mixed-up.

Remember, however, the assumptions about anxiety as the motivating force of what we do and the adaptive-maladaptive distinction. An absolute consistency among levels produces rigidity. That very constancy limits our adjustment to only one part of our environment, a dangerously maladaptive pattern. A sharp contradiction among levels brings conflict and chaos. That very changeableness unleashes a frantic attempt to adjust to every part of the environment at once, also a dangerously maladaptive pattern.

Some difference among levels is necessary for growth. Some similarity among levels is desirable for maturity.

Reciprocal Behavior

Because we are not human by ourselves, how we act toward others is intimately and inevitably bound up with how others act toward us. That is, I become who I am in large part because of the kinds of experiences I have with people who are significant for me. They affect me and I, in turn, affect them.

We tend to build up particular patterns of relating that take on a high degree of consistency. We develop ways of acting that have the probability of producing the kinds of response from others that are likely to keep our anxiety reduced and our sense of well-being enhanced.[11]

In fact, a key way of understanding what goes on between individuals is to view their interpersonal behavior as reciprocal. Each person attempts through the way he acts "to establish an emotional state in the interaction which tends to elicit a predictable response from the other person." [12] For instance, if I shove someone, he is likely to shove me back. On the other hand, if I ask for help in a polite manner, the person is likely to try to help me as much as he can. Each of us tends to pull from others the kinds of response that keep his world steady, whether that steadiness be unhealthy rigidity or adaptive constancy.

Groups Similar to Individuals

While groups are made up of individuals, a group always constitutes more than the sum of the individuals involved. The group takes on characteristics and patterns that transcend its particular members. Thus, within a group individuals' experiences and behaviors are modified by the forces operating within the group as group.

Even though groups are distinct from individuals, groups may be understood in terms of the working assumptions I have been outlining for individuals. In relation to other groups, each group acts in such a way as to reduce anxiety and build up its own position. In relation to other groups, each group's activity may be fitting or inappropriate depending upon the setting in which the activity takes place, the time when it occurs, and the intensity of its expression.

A group may be thought of as having various levels to its "personality." [13]

> There is its rationale,
> what it articulates as its basis for being;
>
> there is its organization,
> how it carries on its functioning;
>
> there is its hope,
> what it strives to achieve;
>
> there is its reality,
> what it is willing to live with.

Like an individual, a group is complex, dynamic, and goal-directed.

These five assumptions, then, provide the foundation on which to construct an orienting compass:

> What we do is designed to reduce anxiety and to enhance well-being.
>
> What we do may be adaptive or maladaptive depending on its appropriateness, accuracy, and balance.
>
> The relationship among the various levels of how we act, how we see ourselves, and what are our underlying potentials determines our openness or closedness to the future.
>
> What we are develops from reciprocal patterns between ourselves and others that we find useful for "making it" in the world.
>
> While a group is different from an individual, a group's relationship with other groups may be understood in a way similar to the way we understand interpersonal interactions.

With these as background, we can now turn to an examination of the dynamics of individual and group behavior. We want to transform random change into intelligent change. We prefer responsible change to instant change. What does a usable compass look like?

AGREEMENT ON INTERPERSONAL BEHAVIOR

Investigation during the past twenty years of what takes place between persons has disclosed a remarkable convergence of thinking and results. This has come in spite of the fact that the research has stemmed from different theoretical orientations and different empirical referents. We are finding "a simple ordered structure for the organization of interpersonal behavior." [14] Each interpersonal act serves the dual purpose of "giving or denying love *and* status to the self *and* to the other." [15] When ordered on a circular basis, the two dimensions of relation to oneself and relation to the other are sufficient to describe what goes on in any interpersonal act.

Two-Dimensional Circle

The way we interact with each other, then, can be expressed as a combination of four centering or nodal points.[16] These interacting axes are shown in Figure 1. The vertical axis stands for the dimension of power or the Dominance-Submission factor; the horizontal axis for the dimension of love or the Affiliation-Distance factor.

The power axis constitutes a continuum from dominance to submission. One pole is defined by acts of self-confidence and self-assertiveness, autonomy, and environmental mastery. The other pole expresses acts of passivity and submissiveness, dependence and powerlessness.

The love axis makes up a continuum from affiliation to distance. One pole is defined by warm, friendly acts; the other by critical, hostile acts. This continuum from closeness and identification to distance and identity is regarded as basic to all human learning.[17]

Each act, thereby, reflects the degree of acceptance or rejection of oneself in terms of power *and* the degree of acceptance or rejection of the other in terms of love. In understanding what goes on between people, we try to locate on the vertical axis whether a response is dominant or submissive and on the horizonal axis whether it is affiliative or distant. Each perspective emphasizes certain aspects of a response without excluding other aspects. When combined, the perspectives give us a conceptual

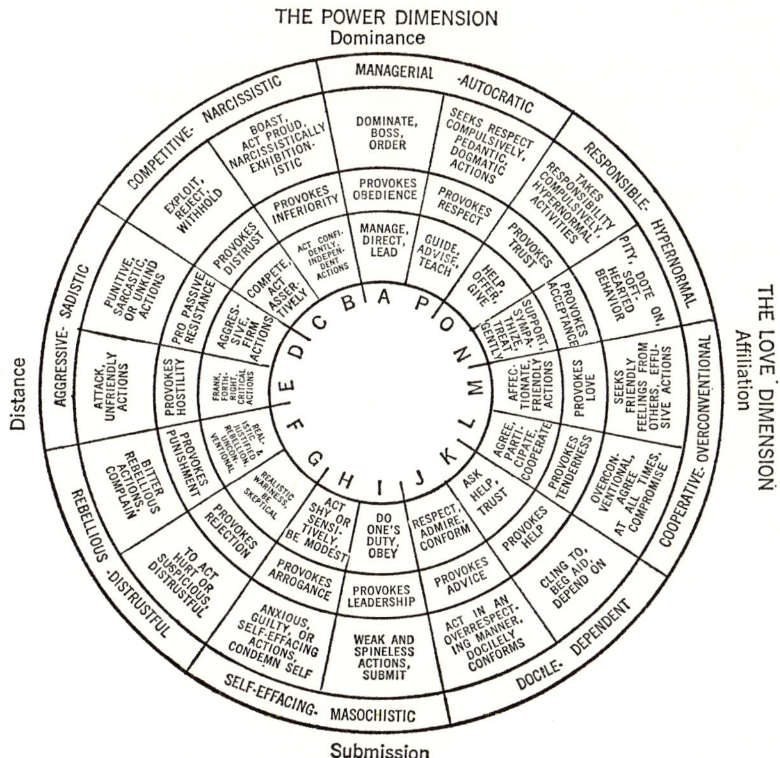

FIGURE 1. Classification of Interpersonal Behavior into Sixteen Mechanisms or Reflexes. Each of the sixteen interpersonal variables is illustrated by sample behaviors. The inner circle presents illustrations of adaptive reflexes, e.g., for the variable **A, manage.** The center ring indicates the type of behavior that this interpersonal reflex tends to "pull" from the other one. Thus we see that the person who uses the reflex **A** tends to provoke others to **obedience,** etc. These findings involve two-way interpersonal phenomena (what the subject does and what the "Other" does back) and are therefore less reliable than the other interpersonal codes presented in this figure. The next circle illustrates extreme or rigid reflexes, e.g., **dominates.** The perimeter of the circle is divided into eight general categories employed in **interpersonal diagnosis.** Each category has **a** moderate (adaptive) and an extreme (pathological) intensity, e.g., **Managerial-Autocratic.**

From Timothy Leary, *Interpersonal Diagnosis of Personality* (New York: The Ronald Press, 1957), p. 65. Used by permission.

framework of an operating system made up of functionally interrelated parts.

Such a basic framework (made systematic by the two-dimensional circular structure) has been "described repeatedly ever since the time of Hippocrates." [18] Unless there were certain universal features in all human conduct, such similarities and convergences would not have appeared with such consistency. Thus, we are dealing here with basic categories descriptive of the ways in which people relate to each other.[19]

4ths, 8ths, 16ths

For a more refined analysis the circle may be viewed in terms of its quadrants. Thus, reading clockwise, we have a dominant-affiliative pattern, an affiliative-submissive pattern, a submissive-hostile pattern, and a hostile-dominant pattern. Psychiatrist Thomas Harris has translated that patterning into four basic positions that are descriptive of the ways in which we interact with each other. Those positions, again reading clockwise are:[20]

"I'm OK—you're not OK" *or* the position of the criminal stance	"I'm OK—you're OK" *or* the response of the mature adult at peace with himself and others
"I'm not OK—you're not OK" *or* the "give-up" position of the despairing	"I'm not OK—you're OK" *or* the anxious dependency of the immature

The circle may be viewed in terms of its octants. Thus, Leary and his colleagues divided two-way interpersonal responses into eight general categories. Look again at Figure 1. If you read clockwise, you find that those behaviors are: Managerial-Autocratic; Responsible-Hypernormal; Cooperative-Overconventional; Docile-Dependent; Self-Effacing-Masochistic; Rebellious-Distrustful; Aggressive-Sadistic; Competitive-Narcissistic. You will note that in line with the adaptive-maladaptive assumption each category has a moderate (adaptive) and an extreme (pathological) intensity; e.g., Responsible-Hypernormal.

For more detailed analysis the circle may also be viewed in terms of sixteen interpersonally oriented behavior categories. In Figure 1 the circle is shown with illustrative sample behaviors.

By coupling the letters and verbs we can read them clockwise as: AP—manage/guide; ON—help/support; ML—affectionate actions/cooperate; KJ—trust/admire; IH—do one's duty/act shy; GF—wariness/rebellion; ED—frank/aggressive; CB—compete/act confidently.

The various types of dominant-supportive behavior (AP-NO) are mixtures of strong and close orientations to others. Distrustful behaviors (FG-HI) appear to blend hostility and weakness. The difficulty with these behaviors is the seemingly positive value of the first four combinations and the seemingly negative value of the second four combinations. I shall return to that shortly, but for the moment let it stand.

Figure 1 shows systematically the types of response various behaviors are intended to provoke from others. Undoubtedly you will find the exposition that follows complicated. It makes assumptions that space does not allow me to explain and so you will have to take it at face value. There is little of the concrete to awaken your interest. As you become more familiar with the reciprocal patterns of interpersonal relationships, you will find yourself referring to this with increasing understanding and insight.

The Distrustful Personality, who reduces anxiety by rebellion, pulls from others punitive rejection and superiority, e.g., FG provokes BCD.[21] He is weak and hostile. The Masochistic Personality, who reduces anxiety through self-effacement, pulls from others depreciation and superiority, e.g., HI provokes BC and DE.[22] He is withdrawn.

The Dependent Personality, who reduces anxiety through docility, pulls from others strong helpful leadership, e.g., JK provokes AP and NO.[23] He is weak and friendly. The Overly Conventional Personality, who reduces anxiety through cooperation, pulls from others approval, e.g., LM provokes MN.[24] He is bland.

The Hypernormal Personality, who reduces anxiety through responsibility, pulls from others dependency, e.g., NO provokes KL.[25] He is friendly and strong. The Autocratic Personality, who reduces anxiety through power, pulls from others obedience, deference, and respect, e.g., AP provokes IJ.[26] He is strong and neutral.

The Narcissistic Personality, who reduces anxiety through competition, pulls from others envy, distrust, inferiority, and respectful admiration, e.g., BC provokes GHIJ.[27] He is strong and hostile. The Sadistic Personality, who reduces anxiety through aggression, pulls from others resentment, distrust, fear, and guilt, e.g., DE provokes FGH.[28] He is alienated and strong.

The more manipulative and maladaptive a person is the more power he has to control our relationship with him.[29] He has fewer behavioral responses available for the interaction. These few responses take on more and more power with greater and greater rigidity.

The healthier a person is the more wholesome and satisfying his relationships are. He has many responses available for the interaction. So he exercises a freedom, a spontaneity, and a fullness in moving into relationships and meeting life face-to-face.

We now have an orienting compass. Four nodal variables appear to be the minimum number required to understand interpersonal behavior, while sixteen basic variables apparently are the maximum number for an optimal degree of refinement. What goes on between people and groups is not as strange and mysterious as we have believed it to be. There is some sense, order, and pattern to what we do.

Thirteen

What Does Go On?

The previously suggested compass gives an orientation and the suggested map includes almost everything. The application of these tools can be made specific by using them for the study of, first, interpersonal patterns and, second, intergroup patterns. By separating these, we may see constancy and change more clearly.

BETWEEN INDIVIDUALS

Consider first the perspective of power. Here is the status attributed to oneself and to others. The axis, shown in Figure 1, moves between the dominant pole on top and the submissive pole on the bottom.

At the dominant pole adaptive behavior would include managing, directing, leading, and teaching. Maladaptive behavior would consist of dominating, bossing, ordering, and dogmatism.

At the submissive pole adaptive behavior includes sensitivity, doing one's duty, respecting, admiring, and fitting in. Maladaptive submission means self-effacing actions, self-condemnation, weak and spineless actions, and overly respectful docility.

Consider next the perspective of love. Here is the acceptance attributed to oneself and to others. The axis, shown in Figure 1, moves between the affiliation pole on the right and the distance pole on the left.

At the affiliation pole adaptive behavior would include agreeable participation, affectionate and friendly actions, support, and sympathy. Maladaptive affiliation would consist of overly-conventional and overly-agreeable responses, effusive actions, and sentimental and soft-hearted behavior.

At the distance pole adaptive behavior includes bluntness, frankness, and appropriate criticalness. Confrontation such as this is usually experienced as hostility by the recipients, even though it may not always be offered with any personal vindictiveness. Maladaptive distance involves hostility and does mean bitterness, unfriendly attacks, punitive and sadistic actions, and exploitation.

The compass can be applied to understanding maladaptive and manipulative patterns in which all individuals engage. These maladaptive or manipulative patterns are exaggerated behavioral responses that are designed to restrict the aliveness in personal relationships. An individual thereby misuses potentially constructive interactions in ways that tend to be defeating for oneself and for others. In contrast, adaptive or actualizing behavior means appropriate, accurate, and balanced interacting responses that facilitate the unique potentiality of each person.

Figure 2 shows eight manipulative types as outlined by Everett Shostrom.[1] The dictator, calculator, bully, judge, weakling, clinging vine, nice guy, and protector are all manipulators. Each one performs his special art of scheming for a purpose.

The dictator overdoes his strength. He dominates, bosses, orders around, and does everything that enables him to control others. His behavior is designed to provoke obedience to bolster his position.

The calculator exaggerates his management of a situation. By cleverness and shrewdness he outwits and outshines others. His behavior is designed to provoke a feeling of inferiority in others in order to enhance his sense of mastery.

The bully magnifies his aggression. By unkindness and cruelty he humiliates and crushes others. His behavior is intended to provoke hostility, which then justifies his aggressiveness.

The judge heightens his critical attitude. By distrust and blame he puts others on the defensive. His behavior seeks to provoke rejection which, in turn, reinforces his initial skepticism.

The weakling overdoes his uncertainty. By anxiousness and abasement he avoids involvement. His behavior is aimed at pro-

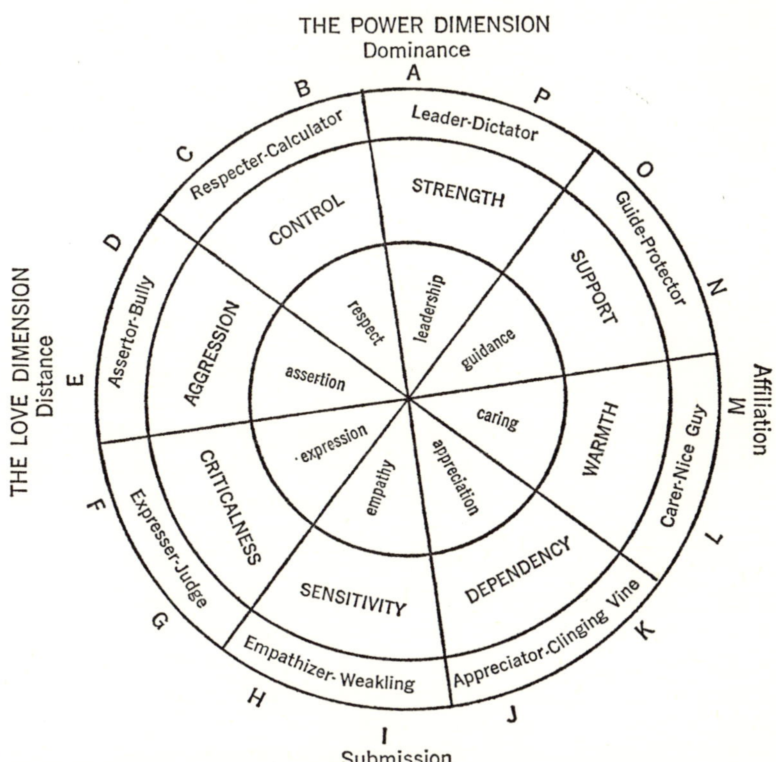

Figure 2. Actualizing and Manipulative Patterns

voking leadership from others in order to free himself from standing out.

The clinging vine exaggerates his dependency. By letting others take over he remains the everlasting child. His behavior is aimed at provoking protective help from others.

The nice guy embroiders friendliness. By effusive warmth he kills with kindness. His behavior seeks to provoke tender affection on the part of others in order to make him feel good.

The protector magnifies his support. By being overly sympathetic and eagerly responsible, he spoils others. His behavior serves the purpose of provoking acceptance of his benevolence and appreciation for his generosity.

Each of these eight patterns reflects a way of keeping the world at a distance. Each is designed to control what others do. Each prevents satisfaction, excitement, and growth. The manipulation may be an active avoiding of weakness by taking on the stance of power, as with the dictator or the calculator. The manipulation may be a passive feigning of helplessness and stupidity in order to be taken care of, as with the weakling or the clinging vine. The manipulation may be a competitive race by battling with others as with the bully or the judge. The manipulation may be an agreeable neutralization in order to avoid conflict, as with the nice guy or the protector. Such neutralization differs from the strategy by the same name discussed by Shostrom.

The result, regardless of how it is arrived at, means withdrawal from genuine relatedness. The individual who engages in one of these manipulations treats others as objects, and so he ends up by treating himself as an object. He behaves casually and coolly. Anger, fear, hurt, trust, and love are blocked. Emotion dies. And when emotion dies, the person dies, too.

Notwithstanding, each of these patterns contains necessary qualities of genuine humanness.[2] Figure 2 also shows eight actualizing types.

Within the domination of the dictator we find the firm direction of real leadership. Within the exploitation of the calculator we come upon the genuine respect for others that flows from genuine respect for one's own capacities. In these qualities of personhood we see an individual who is powerful without overpowering others. One is authentic without becoming autocratic.

Within the aggression of the bully we come upon the straightforward frankness of asserting oneself affirmatively. Within the criticalness of the judge we see the capacity to be realistic about situations. In these potentials of personhood we see an individual who can be critical without being cynical. One is blunt without bludgeoning.

Within the anxiousness of the weakling we come upon the modesty that does one's duty conscientiously. Within the dependency of the clinging vine we find the admiring trust that fosters strength. In these potentials of personhood we see an individual who is unassuming without being self-destructive. One builds others up without tearing oneself down.

Within the gushiness of the nice guy we come upon the cooperative caring that cements relationships. Within the smothering paternalism of the protector we find the responsible guidance that encourages direction. In these potentials of personhood we see an individual who can conserve the values in what is, while creatively fostering what might be. One identifies with others without obscuring individual integrity and potentiality.

Whenever we interact with another (either professionally or personally), these reciprocal patterns operate. By being attuned to our own feelings, we can begin to gauge where the other person is on the compass. From that assessment we can make inferences as to what responses might or might not be fruitful. We can ask ourselves: what is he trying to evoke in me or provoke from me? What implications does the answer have for manipulation or actualization? If I act as he wants me to act, will that foster or frustrate his growth? Can I modify my responses (anger, fear, hurt, trust, love) in order to make contact with him as a person? Can I avoid being manipulated into reacting either as a victim or a victimizer?

Think back to Ronald, who was described in chapter three. When he came, our family wanted to respond with the adaptive behavior of ON, that is, give help in a supportive and gentle way. We expected that he would respond with the adaptive behavior of KJ, that is, would ask help in a trusting and conforming manner. That result never materialized. He came on with the exaggerated EF behavior, that is, bitter rebellion and unfriendly attacks. We, in turn, reacted with the maladaptive CD behavior of rejection and punishment. As he grew more aggressive (ED), we became more bitter and hostile (FE) as well as more anxiously guilty (H).

What we eventually came to was the adaptive stance of firmness and direction (AB). This, in turn, provoked more conforming obedience (IJ). By the time Ronald met his new parents, his trusting and conforming behavior (KJ) was prepared to reciprocate their gentle help (ON).

Or consider the interaction between the junior high worker and girl in chapter five. Her initial request for help came from the lower right quadrant KJ and provoked his helping response from the upper right quadrant ON. As they talked, he shifted his response from the supporting horizontal ON to the more vertical directing AP. By the end of their interview she had moved from the dependency of the lower right JK to the assertive initiative of the upper left quadrant BA.

My interaction with the student in chapter five again illustrates the helpfulness of the circle compass. Jack's passive aggression came from the lower left quadrant FGH. Instead of my responding to the intended provoked behavior of aggressive rejection (DC), I shifted to the direct confrontation of BA. That, in turn, enabled him to shift from the bitterness of the lower left quadrant to the frank assertion of the horizontal E.

Such is the compass and map of what goes on between individuals. And what is the picture between groups?

BETWEEN GROUPS

The two-dimensional circle of power and love is also applicable to our understanding of what goes on between groups.

The most dramatic group interaction within recent years is that between blacks and whites. While the dynamics are similar to those between management and labor, students and professors, or women and men, the attention which the racial crisis has received is greater and that crisis is given more publicity than that of other group interactions. Consequently, I purpose to use the black/white reciprocity as a way to describe and illustrate other group interactions.

Kenneth Clark has characterized eight strategies for change in the civil rights arena.[3] These may be regarded as prototypes of most group strategies for activity that affects intergroup relationships. He has listed them separately, but we can order them according to the power/love axes, as shown in Figure 3. They move counterclockwise on the circle.

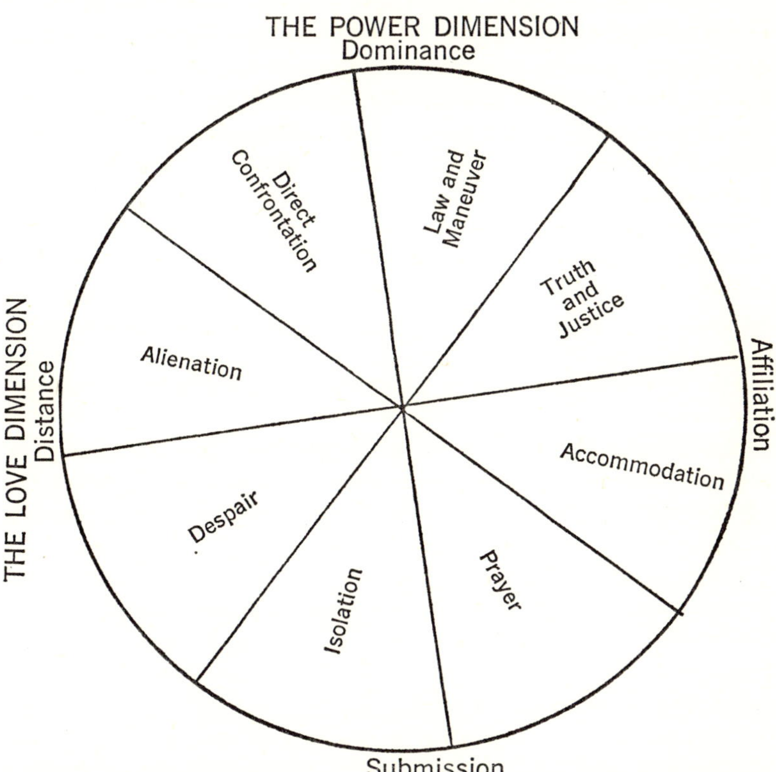

Figure 3. Civil Rights Strategies in the Power/Love Model [4]

The strategy of law and maneuver is primarily the technique which the National Association for the Advancement of Colored People and the National Urban League have used to achieve significant gains by means of constitutional decisions and by political and economic pressures. Occasionally the Southern Christian Leadership Conference also may be characterized in this fashion.

The strategy of direct confrontation is the action pattern of the Congress of Racial Equality, the Student Non-Violent Coordinating Council, and militant student groups. Kenneth Clark has used the expression "direct encounter," which implies affiliative contact. I have used, instead, "direct confrontation," which implies more demanding contact. While the Southern Christian Leadership Conference may seem to fall into this strategy, it more properly is classified under law, maneuver, truth, and justice because of its nonviolent philosophy.

The strategy of alienation is the separatism and resegregation advocated and practiced by the Black Muslims, the Black Nationalists, and the Black Panthers.

The strategy of despair is primarily an abandoning of hope by the poor rural and urban masses.

The strategy of isolation is "employed by a few aristocratic or wealthy Negroes who choose to live apart." It also includes the apathy that represents a deeper stage of hopelessness than despair.

The strategy of prayer has been applied for generations. It is a reliance upon divine intervention and individual solace, with the expectation of little social change. Such posturing sharply contrasts with the more dynamic form of praying, exemplified by the Southern Christian Leadership Conference, that seeks God's help in its efforts to bring about social change.

The strategy of accommodation has been practiced by the Negro middle-class adapters to white values, resulting in the derogatory term "Uncle Tom."

The strategy of truth has been designated by Clark as "the method of the intellectual" seeking through research and writing "to motivate others to achieve social change by the power of eloquent expressions, a fusion of reason and feeling." [5] More appropriately, it may be characterized as the strategy of justice, for in terms of the two axes it combines the autonomous power of the participants with an adaptive identification with the culture for the purpose of establishing humanness and undistorted truth.

Abstractly, the strategy of truth implies the blueprint for an optimal tactic in intergroup relationships. Yet, in dealing with a recalcitrant agency, an openly corrupt body of politicians, an insensitive institutional structure, or other such power groups that respond only to pressure, optimal activity must and does give way to more confrontational modes of interaction as exemplified by the Southern Christian Leadership Conference and, in some instances, the Black Panthers.

When these strategies are translated into the proposed compass of interaction between groups, as suggested in Figure 4, the dynamics become clearer.

When a group experiences strength, it exhibits behavior ranging from confrontation, through autonomy, to collaboration (CB-AP-ON). As that behavior intensifies, it becomes increasingly maladaptive, ending in conflict, arrogance, and paternalism.

When a group experiences affiliation with another group, it exhibits cooperative behavior at best or conformative behavior at worst (ML). In contrast, when it experiences distance, it exhibits either adaptive opposition or maladaptive militancy (DE).

When a group experiences weakness, it exhibits behavior ranging from consensus, through withdrawal, to skepticism (JK-HI-FG). As that behavior intensifies, it becomes increasingly maladaptive, ending up as acquiescence, apathy, and bitterness.

Group tragedies come about when a group (1) moves too swiftly and too intensely to confrontation, thus alienating an agency or institution or individual that could have been persuaded by eloquence, reason, and feeling; or (2) tries continually to persuade by eloquence, reason, and feeling in a situation in which the opponent is gathering ammunition, manning legislative barricades, or barring doors so that exposable corruption or failure is sealed up. To recognize the optimal tactic of justice and collaboration is necessary; to limit a group to that regardless of circumstances is disastrous. It overlooks the adaptive quality of each octant as well as the maladaptive quality.

The compass can be applied to understanding the intense interaction between blacks and whites. In doing so, I must warn that I am distorting the diversity of individual experiences and behaviors. The black community is no more monolithic than the white community. At any one period and with any one group the pattern might be and has been quite different. Ralph Ellison, for

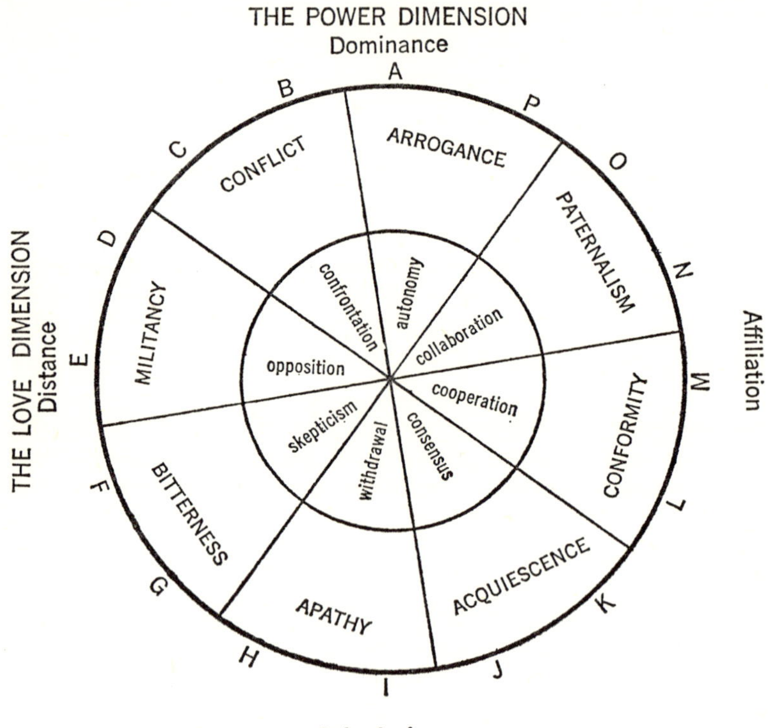

Figure 4. Intergroup Interaction on the Power/Love Model

instance, has noted that he was part of a group of black artists who did *not* regard themselves as self-hating and defensive as

> projected by certain specialists in the "Negro problem." . . . We felt, among ourselves at least, that we were supposed to be whoever we would and could be and do anything and everything which other boys did, and do it better. . . . Because to measure up to our own standards was the only way of affirming our notion of manhood.[6]

At this point I am sketching a broad historical development in order to illustrate the helpfulness of the proposed compass in the understanding of interactions between groups.

If we look at black-white interaction over the past two decades, a discernible pattern emerges. The black community has moved from an affiliative and weak position of black acquiescence (JK), reflected in outward consensus and dependence, into black apathy (HI), seen in their outward withdrawal from white contact and depreciation of themselves. As they began to experience the strength resulting from their struggle to lift their spirits, their behavior erupted in black bitterness (FG), reflected in suspicious antagonism, mushrooming into black power (DE) with its abusive and abrasive resegregation stances.

Once group strength began to be felt, behavior took on the character of black militancy (BC), seen in competitive conflict with whites. Instead of burning down ghetto areas, the militants demanded construction jobs. Instead of absolutely and totally rejecting American (white) culture, they shoved their way through the door. Instead of playing no part in ongoing events, they wanted very much to take part.

As solid gains flowed from confrontation, blacks, in the summer of 1969, began to speak more of dignity than of power. They fought for positions of authority and not merely positions of employment. They continued to reflect a dominating autonomy (BAP), but that kind of behavior stood in stark contrast to earlier and widespread bitter militancy (EFG).

Such behavior patterns have provoked reciprocal patterns from the white community. The white community has tended to move from a strong and affiliative position of white paternalism (ON), reflected in racial blindness and condescension to colored folks, into white domination (AP) and institutional racism, seen in the belief that they were doing "right" by the Negro.

As black bitterness exploded, however, it provoked in whites a more openly competitive bias (BC), seen in racial entrenchment. As conflict spread, white backlash (CDE), with its aggressive clashing, soon collapsed into white fearfulness (GHI), reflected in frustrated bitterness and neurotic guilt. In some instances, it even spread into a white timidity (JK) that meekly went along with whatever blacks demanded. Fortunately, in a few places, as blacks exhibited autonomy, whites again experienced white dignity. Where that occurred a collaborative pattern could take hold.

Figure 5 summarizes the development of black/white interaction at Colgate Rochester/Bexley Hall described in chapter eleven. In each octant label the first term describes the more intense maladaptive response and the second the more appropriate adaptive response, for example, arrogance—autonomy.

While the diversity of the actual phases is obscured, the general pattern is accentuated. If you were to reread that chapter now, both what occurred over the years and the focus of the circle compass would take on more clarity.

No one person symbolizes the broken black more than Malcolm X. As Rosa Parks became a symbol of the weariness of Negroes, so Malcolm X initially was a symbol of the recklessness that extreme weariness can produce.[7] His agonized pilgrimage is now interpreted as the agonized pilgrimage of all blacks in their search for identity. His autobiography lays out the black-white interaction in the United States much as I have characterized it. If we look at his autobiography chapter by chapter, we can begin to fill in details supportive of our orienting compass:[8]

Chapter One: *Nightmare,* the base from which he began. Here he depicts the tragic militancy of his father, the crushed demise of his mother, and his own maladaptive affiliation with the white culture (LKJ).

Chapter Two: *Mascot,* in which he experiences that (1) he is not perceived as a human being, and (2) he is integrated and seeks integration but as a false goal (in retrospect), a maladaptive dependency (KJ).

Chapters Three and Four: *"Homeboy"* and *Laura,* in which he breaks from passive acquiescence into active immersion in black culture. He does so, however, with an unconscious self-rejecting, black-rejecting attitude, a maladaptive masochism. (IH).

Chapters Five through Ten: *Harlemite, Detroit Red, Hustler, Trapped, Caught,* and *Satan,* in which he aggressively distances

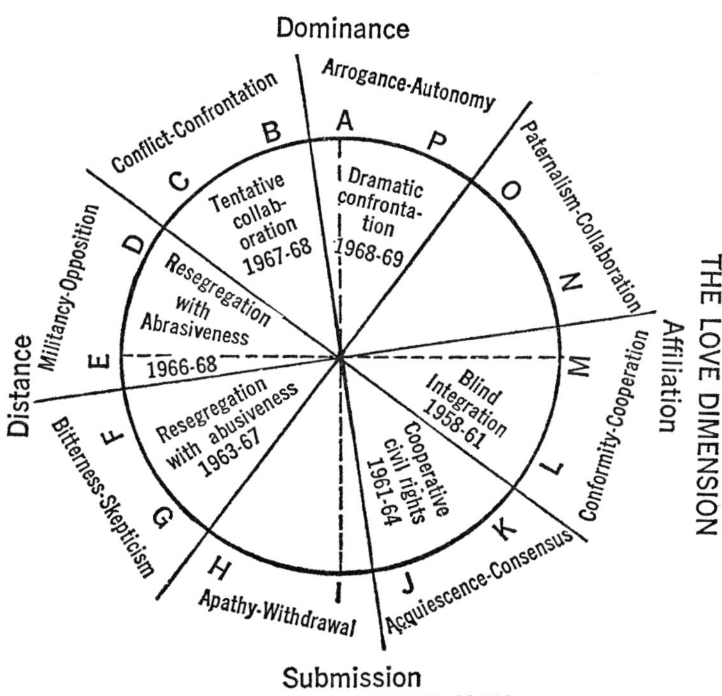

Figure 5. Phases of Black Response at Colgate Rochester/ Bexley Hall 1958-1969 Arranged on the Power/Love Model

himself from white culture. He expresses antagonistic bitterness, condemning both the white devil and the brainwashed black. This represents a more adaptive distrustfulness (GF).

Chapters Eleven through Fourteen: *Saved, Savior, Minister Malcolm X,* and *Black Muslims,* in which increasing self-respect comes from a disciplined devotion to black separatism and black supremacy. He is openly angry with and militant against everything and anything white, a more adaptive assertiveness (ED).

Chapters Fifteen through Eighteen: *Icarus, Out, Mecca, El-Hajj Malik El-Shabazz,* in which he begins (1) to see "white" as an attitude more than a people; (2) to give up blanket indictment of whites; (3) to stress black self-sufficiency by means of voting rights and developing a black economic base; and (4) to reorder completely his militancy because of *(a)* disillusionment with Elijah Muhammad, *(b)* conversion to a vision of the oneness of man because of glimpsing the Oneness of God during his pilgrimage to Mecca, and *(c)* the experience of seeing blacks in positions of responsibility in the nonwhite world of the Near East and Africa, an adaptive respectfulness (CB).

Chapter Nineteen: *1965,* in which he (1) stresses truth and justice, spirit and love; (2) claims the Negro's so-called "revolt" is "not trying to overturn the system or to destroy it" but "is merely an asking to be *accepted* into the existing system"; (3) takes a second look at all his previous attitudes and opens himself to previously unthinkable possibilities (such as interracial marriage); and (4) affirms the humanity of human beings beyond the particulars of race, an adaptive firmness (APO).

Malcolm X's development displays the same clockwise movement as the behavior of blacks in general over the last twenty years. It reinforces the point that from a sense of worthlessness arises bitter anger. From bitter anger there comes a growing sense of militancy and power. With increasing power there appears more desire to attain evidences of worth based upon the advantages of the existing culture. With experiences of worth combined with experiences of power one tends to participate more directly in the mainstream of culture. This participation, however, is not an uncritical accommodation but rather a critical constructiveness that seeks to enable the system to function optimally for everyone.

The last period of Malcolm X's growth covered only the nine months from May, 1964, until February, 1965. The newly conceived life had just about enough time to be born. With his assassination, it was ended just at the time when it was beginning. Yet the direction stands forth clear and focused. By his finding his way toward all humanity, so he is making it possible for others to find their way. As time goes on, the significance of his pilgrimage will dawn upon whites even as it has already dawned upon blacks.

The Constant Dilemma

No single way will be adequate to construe interpersonal and intergroup behaviors. They are patterned but also particular. They may be identified but are also idiosyncratic. Notwithstanding, without some sense of what does go on, we are left at the mercy of a chaotic, irrational, and arbitrary environment.

I have suggested an orienting compass based upon the interpenetration of power and love. The power dimension runs vertically from positions of dominance and strength to positions of submission and sensitivity. The love dimension runs horizontally from positions of closeness and identification to positions of distance and identity. The working assumptions of anxiety reduction, adaptive-maladaptive intensity, levels of analysis, and reciprocity of behavior patterns, on which the compass is based, apply to both interpersonal and intergroup relationships.

But the dilemma between how much constancy and how much change continues. Whether we are dealing with an individual or with a group, both the dimension of power and the dimension of love pose problems.

The dimension of power deals with achievement, impersonal tasks, and the ways in which we handle reality. It is the continuum that connects submission to the forces of life with assertion in shaping the forms of life. Here is change. Because of it, we struggle constantly with the questions:

When do we *give up* what is achieved for what is potential? When do we sacrifice what is secure for what is unknown?

When do we *risk* what is possible for what is real? When do we hang on to what is feasible and let go of what is desirable? [9]

The dimension of love deals with the personal, our associations, and the ways in which we relate to each other. It is the continuum that connects us with our world and our world with us. Here is constancy. Because of it, we grapple constantly with the questions:

How much of the world *can we take in* without destroying our individuality?

What of the world *must we take in* if we are to avoid an empty identity? [10]

As I come to the end of this book, I experience some frustration. I have shared a variety of experiences and an increasingly systematized frame of reference with which to orient and organize life. After finishing these last two chapters of a technical nature, you may be asking yourself the question: *"So what? Now that you have a map and a compass, do they really make as much difference as you claim they do? Does all this elaboration substantially help you with the real tension between constancy and change? You have been able to illustrate its use in retrospect, but can it be fruitful in the midst of concrete situations or in strategizing how to move in concrete situations?"*

In John Steinbeck's delightful account of his search to rediscover America, he describes the ambiguity of maps. They can help us along the way, yet they can equally get in the way. Here is what he says:

> For weeks I had studied maps, large-scale and small, but maps are not reality at all—they can be tyrants. I know people who are so immersed in road maps that they never see the countryside they pass through, and others who, having traced a route, are held to it as though held by flanged wheels to rails.[11]

I'm not certain how to respond to that kind of concern. I have labored over a map. Now I propose that we both forget it. I have written *of* change and I have reflected *about* change. What matters now is neither my experience nor my reflection.

You have your experience to pass through and to reflect upon. Do not miss your reality by confusing my map with Reality. Periodically you may want to check your experience with my map to see if it helps you get your bearings. If it helps you to continue on your journey, well enough. If it doesn't, then leave it and construct your own kind of guidance. Then perhaps we can compare experiences for the sake of more effective ministry and deepened life.

Notes

having-to-be-in-this-world

[1] D. H. Lawrence, *Lady Chatterley's Lover*, with an introduction by Mark Schorer (New York: Grove Press, Inc., 1964), p. 3.

WHY THIS BOOK?

[1] Palma Bucarelli, *Giacometti* (Rome: Editalia-Edizioni d'Italia, 1962), p. 14.

[2] *Ibid.*, p. 44.

[3] *Ibid.*, pp. 66, 68.

[4] See Alvin Toffler, *Future Shock* (New York: Random House, Inc., 1970). I am indebted to Phyllis Stein for calling this work to my attention.

[5] Theodore Roszak, *The Making of a Counter Culture: Reflections on the Technocratic Society and Its Youthful Opposition* (Garden City, N.Y.: Doubleday & Company, Inc., 1969), p. 96.

[6] *Ibid.*, pp. 96-97.

CHAPTER ONE

[1] John Steinbeck, *Travels with Charley: In Search of America* (New York: The Viking Press, Inc., 1962), p. 30.

[2] Cf. Alvin Toffler, *Future Shock* (New York: Random House, Inc., 1970).

[3] Stephen Neill, *A Genuinely Human Existence* (Garden City, N.Y.: Doubleday & Company, Inc., 1959), p. 108.

[4] 1 John 3:2; see Isaiah 48:6-7; see 1 Corinthians 13:12.

[5] Gordon W. Allport, *Pattern and Growth in Personality* (New York: Holt, Rinehart & Winston, Inc., 1961), p. 20.

[6] Dietrich Bonhoeffer, *Letters and Papers from Prison*, ed. Eberhard Bethge and trans. Reginald H. Fuller (New York: The Macmillan Company, 1962).

able-to-be-in-this-world

[1] Simone Weil, *Waiting for God,* trans. Emma Craufurd (New York: G. P. Putnam's Sons, 1951), p. 115.

CHAPTER TWO

[1] Frederick H. Allen, *Psychotherapy with Children* (New York: W. W. Norton & Company, Inc., 1942), pp. 129-130.

[2] Cf. Anna Freud, *The Psychoanalytical Treatment of Children* (New York: Schocken Books, Inc., 1946).

[3] Allen, *op. cit.*

[4] *Ibid.,* p. 52.

[5] *Ibid.,* p. 295.

[6] Fritz Redl and David Wineman, *Children Who Hate* (Glencoe, Ill.: The Free Press, 1951); *Controls from Within* (Glencoe, Ill.: The Free Press, 1952).

[7] Redl and Wineman, *Controls from Within,* pp. 12-13. Adapted from the Table of Contents.

CHAPTER THREE

[1] Claude J. G. Montefiore, ed., *The Synoptic Gospels: Edited with an Introduction and a Commentary* (New York: Ktav Publishing House, Inc., 1968), p. 39.

[2] Sidney M. Jourard, *Disclosing Man to Himself* (Princeton: Van Nostrand Reinhold Company, 1968), p. 137.

[3] *Ibid.,* pp. 137-138.

[4] *Ibid.,* p. 149.

[5] Frederick S. Perls, *Gestalt Therapy Verbatim.* Compiled and edited by John O. Stevens (Lafayette, Calif.: Real People Press, 1969), p. 50.

[6] Cf. William C. Schutz, *Joy: Expanding Human Awareness* (New York: Grove Press, Inc., 1967), pp. 107-114. Copyright © 1967 by William C. Schutz and used by permission. Italics mine.

[7] *Ibid.,* p. 114.

[8] Cf. Luke 15:17a; Ephesians 4:18.

[9] Bernard Gunther, *Sense Relaxation: Below Your Mind!* (New York: The Macmillan Company, 1968), pp. 112, 144.

[10] James H. Cone, *Black Theology and Black Power* (New York: The Seabury Press, Inc., 1969), pp. 137-138.

[11] W. E. Burghardt Du Bois, *The Souls of Black Folk: Essays and Sketches* (Chicago: A. C. McClurg & Co., 1904), p. 258. See also Fawcett Premier edition of *The Souls of Black Folk,* 1961.

[12] John L. Sherrill, *They Speak with Other Tongues* (Old Tappan, N.J.: Fleming H. Revell Company, 1965), p. 72. Used with permission of McGraw-Hill Book Company. I am indebted to Ronald Small for calling this work to my attention.

[13] *Ibid.,* pp. 121-123, 132. Italics mine.

[14] Albert Mehrabian, "Communication Without Words," *Psychology Today,* vol. 2, no. 4 (September, 1968), pp. 53-55.

[15] Schutz, *op. cit.,* pp. 25-26.

[16] Rudolf Bultmann, *Theology of the New Testament,* vol. 1, trans. Kendrick Grobel (New York: Charles Scribner's Sons, 1954), pp. 195-196.

[17] *Ibid.,* p. 199.

[18] John 13:35; 1 John 3:14.

[19] Cf. Romans 16:16; 1 Corinthians 16:20; 2 Corinthians 13:12; 1 Thessalonians 5:26.

[20] Carl R. Rogers and Rosalind F. Dymond, eds., *Psychotherapy and Personality Change* (Chicago: The University of Chicago Press, 1954), pp. 328, 332, 339.

[21] Carl R. Rogers, "The Group Comes of Age," *Psychology Today,* vol. 3, no. 7 (December, 1969), p. 58. Material for this article was taken from *Challenges of Humanistic Psychology,* James F. T. Bugental, ed. (New York: McGraw-Hill Book Company, 1967). Used with permission of McGraw-Hill Book Company.

[22] *The New York Times,* July 24, 1968, p. 3. © 1968 by The New York Times Company. Reprinted by permission.

CHAPTER FOUR

[1] Seward Hiltner and Lowell G. Colston, *The Context of Pastoral Counseling* (Nashville: Abingdon Press, 1961), pp. 24-25.

[2] *Ibid.,* pp. 29-31.

[3] *Ibid.,* p. 220.

demonstrating-being-in-this-world

[1] Truman Capote, *The Grass Harp* (New York: Random House, Inc., 1951), pp. 66, 68.

CHAPTER FIVE

[1] Cf. Wayne Dennis, "The Significance of Feral Man"; R. M. Zingg, "Reply to Professor Dennis," *American Journal of Psychology,* vol. 54 (1941), pp. 425-435.

[2] E. Earl Baughman and George S. Welsh, *Personality: A Behavioral Science* (Englewood Cliffs, N.J.: Prentice-Hall, Inc., 1962), pp. 178-179.

[3] *Ibid.,* pp. 180-182.

[4] Harry Stack Sullivan, *The Interpersonal Theory of Psychiatry,* ed. Helen S. Perry and Mary L. Gawel (New York: W. W. Norton & Company, Inc., 1953), p. 32.

[5] William Glasser, *Reality Therapy* (New York: Harper & Row, Publishers, 1965), pp. 5-7.

[6] Ronald Laing, *The Divided Self: An Existential Study in Sanity and Madness* (New York: Pantheon Books, A Division of Random House, Inc., 1960), p. 178.

[7] Cf. Charles B. Truax and Robert R. Carkhuff, *Toward Effective Counseling and Psychotherapy: Training and Practice* (Chicago: Aldine Publishing Company, 1967), pp. 23-143.

[8] *Ibid.,* p. 46.

[9] *Ibid.,* p. 58.

[10] *Ibid.,* p. 32.

[11] *Ibid.,* pp. 116-117.

[12] For a fuller discussion of these ways of relating, see Karen Horney, *Our Inner Conflicts* (New York: W. W. Norton & Company, Inc., 1945); Alan Keith-Lucas, "The Nature of the Helping Process," *The Christian Scholar,* vol. 43, no. 1 (Summer, 1960), pp. 119-127; Carl R. Rogers, *On Becoming a Person* (Boston: Houghton Mifflin Company, 1961).

[13] I am indebted to David E. Dickinson for this verbatim.

[14] Clark E. Moustakas, *Creativity and Conformity* (Princeton: Van Nostrand Reinhold Company, 1967), p. 45.

[15] Robert R. Carkhuff and Bernard G. Berenson, *Beyond Counseling and Therapy* (New York: Holt, Rinehart & Winston, Inc., 1967), pp. 170-171.

[16] Cf. Timothy Leary, *Interpersonal Diagnosis of Personality* (New York: The Ronald Press Company, 1957), pp. 29-30.

[17] Carkhuff and Berenson, *op. cit.*, p. 175.

[18] Moustakas, *op. cit.*, p. 45.

[19] Glasser, *op. cit.*, p. 13.

[20] Genesis 11:31–12:1; Deuteronomy 34:1-9; John 16:7.

[21] Lewis Carroll, *Alice's Adventures in Wonderland* (Washington, D.C.: Judd & Detweiler, Inc., 1932), p. 102.

CHAPTER SIX

[1] Cf. Donald S. Williamson, "A Study of Selective Inhibition of Aggression by Church Members," *The Journal of Pastoral Care*, vol. 21, no. 4 (December, 1967), pp. 193-208.

[2] *Ibid.*, p. 193.

[3] Cf. Eugen Rosenstock-Huessy, *The Christian Future or The Modern Mind Outrun* (New York: Charles Scribner's Sons, 1946), p. 19.

CHAPTER SEVEN

[1] T. R. Bennett, "The Layman's Understanding of the Ministry," in Samuel Southard (chairman), *Conference on Motivation for the Ministry* (Louisville, Kentucky: Southern Baptist Theological Seminary, 1959), pp. 72-82.

[2] John Casteel, ed., *Spiritual Renewal Through Personal Groups* (New York: Association Press, 1957), p. 30.

[3] D. Mackenzie Brown, *Ultimate Concern: Tillich in Dialogue* (New York: Harper & Row, Publishers, 1965), pp. 110-111.

[4] Cf. Fred E. Fiedler, *A Theory of Leadership Effectiveness* (New York: McGraw-Hill Book Company, 1967), p. 31; "Style or Circumstance: The Leadership Enigma," *Psychology Today*, vol. 2, no. 10 (March, 1969), pp. 38-43.

CHAPTER EIGHT

[1] Cf. Robert Lee, "The Organizational Dilemma in American Protestantism," *Union Seminary Quarterly Review*, vol. 16, no. 1 (November, 1960), p. 10.

[2] *Ibid.*

[3] Cf. Reuel Howe, *Man's Need and God's Action* (New York: The Seabury Press, Inc., 1953).

[4] Romans 12:4-5, NEB; cf. 1 Corinthians 12:14-31.

[5] Chris Argyris, in Mason Haire, ed., *Modern Organizational Theory* (New York: John Wiley & Sons, Inc., 1959), p. 125.

[6] Haire, *op. cit.*, pp. 185-186.

[7] Cf. Walter F. Buckley, *Sociology and Modern Systems Theory* (Englewood Cliffs, N.J.: Prentice-Hall, Inc., 1967), pp. 14-15.

[8] Cf. Haire, *op. cit.*, pp. 273ff.

[9] The problem of too rapid growth in church life is discussed in Donald F. Metz, *New Congregations: Security and Mission in Conflict* (Philadelphia: The Westminster Press, 1967).

[10] Walter F. Buckley, ed., *Modern Systems Research for the Behavioral Scientist: A Sourcebook* (Chicago: Aldine Publishing Company, 1968), p. 495.

[11] Cf. *Ibid.*, pp. xviii-xx.

[12] Cf. H. Richard Niebuhr, *The Purpose of the Church and Its Ministry* (New York: Harper & Row, Publishers, 1956).

[13] See Philip Selznick, *Leadership in Administration* (New York: Harper & Row, Publishers, 1957).

[14] James E. Dittes, *The Church in the Way* (New York: Charles Scribner's Sons, 1967), p. 12.

[15] Cf. James B. Ashbrook, "The Relationship of Church Members to Church Organization," *Journal for the Scientific Study of Religion,* vol. 5, no. 3 (Fall, 1966), pp. 397-419.

[16] Cf. Bernard Berelson and Gary A. Steiner, *Human Behavior: An Inventory of Scientific Findings* (New York: Harcourt Brace Jovanovich, Inc., 1964), p. 358.

[17] Cf. Paul Tillich, *A History of Christian Thought,* ed. Carl. E. Braaten (New York: Harper & Row, Publishers, Inc., 1968), pp. 40-41.

[18] Cf. Paul Watzlawick, Janet H. Beavin, and Don D. Jackson, *Pragmatics of Human Communication: A Study of Interactional Patterns, Pathologies, and Paradoxes* (New York: W. W. Norton & Company, Inc., 1967).

[19] Buckley, *Modern Systems Research . . .,* p. 500.

[20] Cf. Roger John Williams, *You Are Extraordinary* (New York: Random House, Inc., 1967).

[21] Cf. James B. Ashbrook, "Some Implications of Perceptual-Judgment Preferences in Ministers," Unpublished manuscript, 1967.

[22] Cf. James B. Ashbrook, "Ministerial Leadership and Church Organization," *Ministry Studies,* vol. 1, no. 1 (1967), pp. 22, 29.

[23] Frederick R. Kling, "Value Structures and the Minister's Purpose," in *The Minister's Own Mental Health,* ed., Wayne E. Oates (Great Neck, N.Y.: Channel Press, Inc., 1961), pp. 51-64.

[24] John Macquarrie, *Principles of Christian Theology* (New York: Charles Scribner's Sons, 1966), p. 103. See also pp. 183-184, 310-311.

[25] Cf. William H. Whyte, Jr., *The Organization Man* (New York: Simon & Schuster, Inc., 1956), p. 397.

[26] Cf. Dittes, *op. cit.*

[27] Cf. Philip A. Anderson, *Church Meetings That Matter* (Philadelphia: United Church Press, 1965. Pages 47-58 present an extended discussion of evaluation and an evaluation form. Clyde H. Reid, *Groups Alive-Church Alive* (New York: Harper & Row, Publishers, 1968), p. 60, presents a simpler evaluation sheet.

[28] Cf. Ashbrook, "Ministerial Leadership . . .," pp. 24-27.

responding-to-being-in-this-world

[1] Martin Buber, "Distance and Relation," *Psychiatry,* vol. 20, no. 2 (1957), p. 104.

[2] Eugen Rosenstock-Huessy, *The Christian Future* (New York: Charles Scribner's Sons, 1963), p. xli.

CHAPTER NINE

[1] Cf. Don Browning, "Pastoral Care and Public Ministry," *Christian Century,* vol. 83, no. 39 (September 28, 1966), p. 1177.

[2] Cf. Edgar H. Schein and Warren G. Bennis, *Personal and Organizational Change Through Group Methods: The Laboratory Approach* (New York: John Wiley & Sons, Inc., 1965), pp. 201-203.

[3] See Milton Greenblatt, Paul E. Emery, and Bernard C. Glueck, Jr., eds.,

Poverty and Mental Health (Psychiatric Research Report #21, The American Psychiatric Association, January, 1967).

[4] *Ibid.,* p. 64.

[5] Cf. Leland P. Bradford, Jack R. Gibb, and Kenneth D. Benne, *T-Group Theory and Laboratory Method* (New York: John Wiley & Sons, Inc., 1964).

[6] "The Boston Marathon," *Newsweek,* January 13, 1969, p. 60.

[7] Cf. L. Deckle McLean, "Psychotherapy for Houston Police," *Ebony,* October, 1968, pp. 76-82.

[8] Cf. James B. Ashbrook, "The Small Structured Group as an Instrument in Personal Growth and Organizational Change," *Journal of Pastoral Care,* vol. 24, no. 3 (September, 1970), pp. 178-192.

[9] William Glasser, *Reality Therapy* (New York: Harper & Row, Publishers, 1965), pp. 27-41.

[10] Cf. William Glasser, *Schools Without Failure* (New York: Harper & Row, Publishers, 1969); William Glasser, "The Effect of School Failure on the Life of a Child," Parts 1 and 2, *The National Elementary Principal,* vol. 49, no. 1 (September, 1969), pp. 8-18; vol. 49, no. 2 (November, 1969), pp. 12-18.

[11] William Glasser, *Schools Without Failure,* pp. 132-134.

[12] *Ibid.,* p. 128.

[13] *Ibid.,* pp. 134, 138.

CHAPTER TEN

[1] Kenneth B. Clark, *Dark Ghetto: Dilemma of Social Power.* Foreword by Gunnar Myrdal (New York: Harper & Row, Publishers, 1965), p. 232.

[2] *Ibid.,* p. 236.

[3] *Ibid.,* p. 237.

[4] *Cf.* Howard J. Clinebell, Jr., *Understanding and Counseling the Alcoholic Through Religion and Psychology* (Nashville: Abingdon Press, 1956).

[5] Robert W. Terry, *For Whites Only* (Grand Rapids, Mich.: William B. Eerdmans Publishing Company, and Detroit, Mich.: Detroit Industrial Mission, 1970), pp. 55-56.

[6] *Ibid.,* p. 20.

[7] *Ibid.,* p. 15.

CHAPTER ELEVEN

[1] William H. Grier and Price M. Cobbs, *Black Rage* (New York: Basic Books, Inc., Publishers, 1968), p. 38.

[2] *The New York Times,* June 14, 1970, "The Week in Review," Section 4, p. 2. © 1970 by The New York Times Company. Reprinted by permission.

[3] *Ibid.*

[4] Eldridge Cleaver, *Soul on Ice.* Introduction by Maxwell Geismar (New York: Dell Publishing Co., Inc., 1968), p. 3. Copyright © 1968 McGraw-Hill Book Company.

[5] Grier and Cobbs, *op. cit.,* pp. 23-38, 66.

[6] Cf. C. Eric Lincoln, *My Face Is Black* (Boston: Beacon Press, 1964), p. 37.

[7] Kenneth Clark, *Dark Ghetto: Dilemmas of Social Power* (New York: Harper & Row, Publishers, 1965), p. 11.

[8] Grier and Cobbs, *op. cit.,* pp. 201-202.

[9] Malcolm X, *The Autobiography of Malcolm X*. With the assistance of Alex Haley. Introduction by M. S. Handler. Epilogue by Alex Haley (New York: Grove Press, Inc., 1964), p. 269. Copyright © 1964 by Alex Haley and Malcolm X. Copyright © 1965 by Alex Haley and Betty Shabazz.

[10] Grier and Cobbs, *op. cit.,* p. 58.

[11] Clark, *op. cit.,* p. 194.

[12] *Ibid.,* p. 15.

[13] Malcolm X, *op. cit.,* p. 381.

[14] For the basis of this content analysis, see R. A. Brody, "Some Systematic Effects of the Spread of Nuclear Weapons Technology: A Study Through Simulation of a Multi-nuclear Future," *Journal of Conflict Resolution,* vol. 7, no. 4 (1963), pp. 663-753.

CHAPTER TWELVE

[1] William Shakespeare, *Antony and Cleopatra,* act 2. sc. 1, lines 41-49. From *Shakespeare: Twenty-Three Plays and the Sonnets,* edited by Parrot, Hubler, and Telfer (New York: Charles Scribner's Sons, 1953).

[2] Gerhard Adler, *The Living Symbol: A Case Study in the Process of Individuation* (New York: Pantheon Books, Inc., Bollingen Series LXIII, 1961), p. 95.

[3] *Ibid.*

[4] Cf. James B. Ashbrook, "The Search for a Usable Image: One Way of Conceiving of Man and His World," *Foundations* (July-September, 1970), pp. 207-220.

[5] Cf. Rollo May, *The Meaning of Anxiety* (New York: The Ronald Press Company, 1950).

[6] Cf. Harry Stack Sullivan, *The Interpersonal Theory of Psychiatry* (New York: W. W. Norton & Co., Inc., 1953).

[7] Cf. Hans Selye, *The Stress of Life* (New York: McGraw-Hill Book Company, 1956).

[8] Abraham Maslow, *Toward a Psychology of Being* (Princeton, N.J.: Van Nostrand Reinhold Company, 1962), pp. 45-49.

[9] Cf. Carl Jung, *Psychological Types: The Psychology of Individuation,* trans. H. Gordon Baynes (New York: Harcourt Brace Jovanovich, Inc., 1946); Stephen Neill, *A Genuinely Human Existence* (New York: Doubleday & Company, Inc., 1958).

[10] Timothy Leary, *Interpersonal Diagnosis of Personality* (New York: The Ronald Press Company, 1957), pp. 40-42. Italics mine.

[11] *Ibid.,* pp. 91-105, 109-112, 115-130.

[12] William J. Mueller, "Patterns of Behavior and Their Reciprocal Impact in the Family and in Psychotherapy," *Journal of Counseling Psychology,* vol. 16, no. 2 (March, 1969), Part 2, monograph, p. 8.

[13] Phale Hale, Thomas Troeger, Gary Bryant, and Michael Scrogin. Seminar at Colgate Rochester/Bexley Hall, October 9, 1969.

[14] Uriel G. Foa, "Convergences in the Analysis of the Structure of Interpersonal Behavior," *Psychological Review,* vol. 68, no. 5 (1961), p. 341.

[15] *Ibid.,* p. 351.

[16] Leary, *op. cit.,* p. 64.

[17] Edgar H. Schein and Warren G. Bennis, *Personal and Organization Change Through Group Methods: The Laboratory Approach* (New York: John Wiley & Sons, Inc., 1965), pp. 272-274.

[18] Henry B. Adams, " 'Mental Illness' or Interpersonal Behavior?" *American Psychologist,* vol. 19, no. 3 (March, 1964), p. 195.

[19] *Ibid.,* pp. 191-197.

[20] Thomas A. Harris, *I'm OK—You're OK: A Practical Guide to Transactional Analysis* (New York: Harper & Row, Publishers, 1969), pp. 47-53.

[21] Leary, *op. cit.,* pp. 269-281.

[22] *Ibid.,* pp. 282-291.

[23] *Ibid.,* pp. 292-302.

[24] *Ibid.,* pp. 303-314.

[25] *Ibid.,* pp. 315-322.

[26] *Ibid.,* pp. 323-331.

[27] *Ibid.,* pp. 332-340.

[28] *Ibid.,* pp. 341-350.

[29] *Ibid.,* p. 126.

CHAPTER THIRTEEN

[1] Everett L. Shostrom, *Man, the Manipulator: The Inner Journey from Manipulation to Actualization* (Nashville: Abingdon Press, 1967). Copyright © 1967 by Abingdon Press. The internal dimensions of this figure are adapted from Timothy Leary, *Interpersonal Diagnosis of Personality* (New York: The Ronald Press Company, 1957). Used by permission.

[2] *Ibid.,* pp. 36-39.

[3] Kenneth Clark, *Dark Ghetto: Dilemmas of Social Power* (New York: Harper & Row, Publishers, 1965), pp. 220-222.

[4] *Ibid.,* pp. 220-221. Strategies adapted from Clark and rearranged.

[5] *Ibid.,* p. 221.

[6] Ralph Ellison, *Shadow and Act* (New York: Random House, Inc., 1964), p. xvii. I am indebted to John David Cato for calling this work to my attention.

[7] Cf. C. Eric Lincoln, *My Face Is Black* (Boston: Beacon Press, 1964), pp. 29-30.

[8] Malcolm X, *The Autobiography of Malcolm X* (New York: Grove Press, Inc., 1964), summary of entire book.

[9] Paul Tillich, *Systematic Theology: Life and the Spirit; History and the Kingdom of God,* vol. 3 (Chicago: The University of Chicago Press, 1963), pp. 41-44.

[10] *Ibid.,* p. 268.

[11] John Steinbeck, *Travels with Charley: In Search of America* (New York: The Viking Press, Inc., 1962), pp. 22-23.